# SCHAUM'S *Easy* OUTLINES

# BASIC ELECTRICITY

# Other Books in Schaum's Easy Outline Series Include:

SCHAUM'S *Easy* OUTLINES

# BASIC ELECTRICITY

BASED ON SCHAUM'S *Outline of*
*Basic Electricity*
BY MILTON GUSSOW

ABRIDGEMENT EDITOR
WILLIAM T. SMITH

SCHAUM'S OUTLINE SERIES
McGRAW-HILL

New York  Chicago  San Francisco  Lisbon  London  Madrid
Mexico City  Milan  New Delhi  San Juan
Seoul  Singapore  Sydney  Toronto

**MILTON GUSSOW** is a principal staff engineer at the Johns Hopkins University Applied Physics Laboratory. He received his B.S. degree with distinction from the U.S. Naval Academy, his B.S.E.E. from the U.S. Navy Postgraduate School, and his M.S. from the Massachusetts Institute of Technology. He has been an adjunct professor at George Washington University, American University, and Johns Hopkins University, where he taught undergraduate and graduate courses in mathematics and electrical engineering. He was formerly Senior Vice President for Education at the McGraw-Hill Continuing Education Center, and he is the author of over seventy technical papers.

**WILLIAM T. SMITH** is associate professor in the department of electrical engineering at the University of Kentucky, where he has taught since 1990 and has twice won the Outstanding Engineering Professor Award. He earned a B.S. from the University of Kentucky and both M.S. and Ph.D. degrees in electrical engineering from the Virginia Polytechnic Institute and State University. During 1999–2000, he was an academic visitor at the IBM Austin Research Laboratory and previously worked as a senior engineer in the Government Aerospace Systems Division of Harris Corporation. He is also co-author of several journal articles and conference papers.

3 4 5 6 7 8 9 0 DOC DOC 0 9 8 7 6 5 4 3

ISBN 0-07-138316-6

*McGraw-Hill*

*A Division of The McGraw-Hill Companies*

# *Contents*

An electric charge has the ability to do work due to the attraction and repulsion caused by the force of its electrostatic field. The ability to do work is called *potential*. When one charge differs from another, there must be a potential difference between them. The sum of potential differences in the electrostatic field is referred to as the *electromotive force (emf )*.

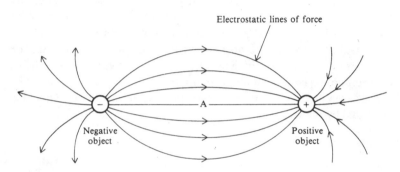

Electrostatic lines of force

Negative object

A

Positive object

**Figure 1-1** The electrostatic field between two opposite charges

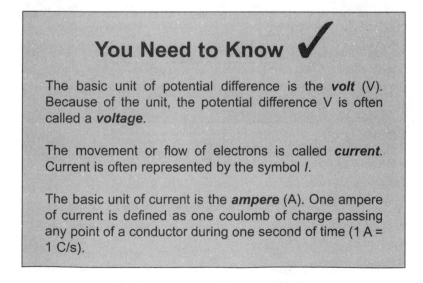

# You Need to Know ✔

The basic unit of potential difference is the *volt* (V). Because of the unit, the potential difference V is often called a *voltage*.

The movement or flow of electrons is called *current*. Current is often represented by the symbol *I*.

The basic unit of current is the *ampere* (A). One ampere of current is defined as one coulomb of charge passing any point of a conductor during one second of time (1 A = 1 C/s).

# 4 BASIC ELECTRICITY

**Example 1.1** If a current of 2 A flows through a point in a conductor for 1 minute, how many coulombs pass through the conductor?

**Solution:** 2 A is 2 coulombs per second (C/s). Since there are 60 s in 1 minute, 60 x 2 = 120 coulombs pass through the conductor.

In a conductor, such as copper wire, free electrons are charges that move with relative ease with an applied potential difference (Figure 1-2). The applied voltage of the battery creates a drift of electrons from the point of the negative charge, $-Q$, at one end of the wire, moving through the wire, and returning to the positive charge, $+Q$, at the other end. The solid arrow (Figure 1-2) indicates the direction of current in terms of electron flow. The direction of moving positive charges, opposite from the electron flow, is considered the **conventional flow** of current and is indicated by the dashed arrow.

**Figure 1-2** Potential difference across two ends of a wire

In basic electricity, circuits are generally evaluated in terms of the conventional flow and that definition is used in this book.

(–) of electricity. The electrons in the outermost shell are called *valence* electrons. When external energy such as heat, light or electric energy is applied to certain materials, the electrons gain energy and can move to a higher energy level. If enough energy is applied, some of the outermost valence electrons will leave the atom as *free electrons*. It is the movement of the free electrons that provides electric current in metal conductors.

Since some atoms lose electrons and others gain electrons, it is possible to cause a transfer of electrons from one object to another. When this takes place, the equal distribution of positive and negative charges in each object no longer exists. The object with excess number of electrons will have a negative (–) electric polarity. The object with deficient number of electrons will have a positive (+) electric polarity. The magnitude of the electric charge is determined by the number of electrons compared with the number of protons in an object. The symbol for the magnitude of electric charge is $Q$ and has units of *coulombs* (C). A charge of –1 C = $6.25 \times 10^{18}$ electrons.

### ☆ Note!

Objects with *like* charges (both positive or negative) repel each other.

Objects with *opposite* charges (one positive, one negative) will attract each other.

The ability of an electric charge to exert a force is due to the presence of an *electrostatic field* surrounding the charged object. The electrostatic field is indicated by lines of force drawn between two objects (Figure 1-1). If an electron is released at point **A** in this field, it will be repelled by the negative charge and attracted by the positive charge. The arrows in Figure 1-1 indicate the direction that would be taken by the electron if it were in different areas of the electric field.

# Chapter 1
# FUNDAMENTALS OF ELECTRICITY AND ELECTRICAL ANALYSIS

IN THIS CHAPTER:

✔ *Electric Charge and Current*
✔ *Electrical Standards and Conventions*
✔ *Graphical Symbols and Schematic Diagrams*
✔ *Ohm's Law and Power*
✔ *Magnetism and Magnetic Fields*
✔ *Electromagnetic Induction*

## Electric Charge and Current

Matter is composed of very small particles called atoms. Atoms are comprised of subatomic particles in various combinations of *electrons, protons,* and *neutrons.* An electron is the fundamental negative charge

The two most common sources for electricity are **batteries** and **generators**.

A voltaic chemical cell is a combination of materials which are used for converting chemical energy into electric energy. A *battery* is formed when two or more cells are connected. A chemical reaction produces opposite charges on two dissimilar metals, which serve as the negative and positive terminals (Figure 1-3).

**Figure 1-3** Voltaic chemical cell

The *generator* is a machine in which electromagnetic inductance is used to produce a voltage by rotating coils of wire through a stationary magnetic field or by rotating a magnetic field through stationary coils of wire. Today, generators produce the majority of electricity.

There are many other sources of electricity including, but not limited to, thermal energy, magnetohydrodynamic (MHD) conversion, thermionic emission, solar cells, piezoelectric effect, photoelectric effect, and thermocouples.

*Direct current* **(dc)** is a current that moves through a conductor or circuit in one direction only.

Unidirectional current flow is produced by direct-current (dc) voltage sources which do not change the polarity of the output voltage (Figure 1-4).

*(a)*                          *(b)*

**Figure 1-4** Waveforms of dc current and voltage

**Note!**

An **alternating-current** (ac) voltage source reverses or alternates polarity periodically .

The resulting current also periodically reverses direction (Figure 1-5). In terms of conventional flow, the current flows from the positive terminal of the voltage source, through the circuit, and back to the negative terminal. When the ac voltage source reverses polarity, the conventional current flows from the negative terminal to the positive.

*(a)*                          *(b)*

**Figure 1-5** Waveforms of ac voltage and current

# Electrical Standards and Conventions

The international system of units or dimensions, commonly called SI, is used in electricity. Table 1-1 shows the basic SI units. Table 1-2 shows the supplementary SI units. Other common units can be derived from the base and supplementary units. For example, the coulomb is derived from the second and the ampere. Table 1-3 shows derived units commonly found in electrical analysis.

### Table 1-1 Base units of the SI system

| Quantity | Base Unit | Symbol |
|---|---|---|
| Length | meter | m |
| Mass | kilogram | kg |
| Time | second | s |
| Electric current | ampere | A |
| Thermodynamic temperature | kelvin | K |
| Light intensity | candela | cd |
| Amount of substance | mole | mol |

### Table 1-2 Supplementary SI Units

| Quantity | Unit | Symbol |
|---|---|---|
| Plane angle | radian | rad |
| Solid angle | steradian | sr |

## Table 1-3 Derived SI Units

| Quantity | Unit | Symbol |
|---|---|---|
| Energy | joule | J |
| Force | newton | N |
| Power | watt | W |
| Electric charge | coulomb | C |
| Electric potential | volt | V |
| Electric resistance | ohm | $\Omega$ |
| Electric conductance | siemens | S |
| Electric capacitance | farad | F |
| Electric inductance | henry | H |
| Frequency | hertz | Hz |
| Magnetic flux | weber | Wb |
| Magnetic flux density | tesla | T |

Often electrical units will provide for numbers that are either very small or very large. Using prefixes on the units is a convenient way to write numbers with large dynamic ranges (Table 1-4). For example, electrical current is often measured in thousandths or millionths of amperes. To illustrate, $1/1000$ A $= 10^{-3}$ A $= 1$ mA (milliampere), $1/1000000$ A $= 10^{-6}$ A $= 1$  A (microampere).

# Graphical Symbols and Schematic Diagrams

A simple electric circuit is shown in pictorial form in Figure 1-6(*a*). The same circuit is drawn in *schematic* form in Figure 1-6(*b*).

## Table 1-4 Metric Prefixes Used in Electricity

| Prefix (Letter Symbol) | Value | |
|---|---|---|
| mega (M) | million | 1 000 000 |
| kilo (k) | thousand | 1 000 |
| milli(m) | thousandth | 0.001 |
| micro (μ) | millionth | 0.000 001 |
| nano (n) | thousand-millionth | 0.000 000 001 |
| pico (p) | million-millionth | 0.000 000 000 001 |

(a) Pictorial diagram                    (b) Schematic diagram

**Figure 1-6** A simple lamp circuit

The *schematic diagram* is a shorthand way to represent an electric circuit. Circuits are usually represented in this symbolic form.

Some standard graphic symbols for commonly used electrical components are given in Figure 1-7. Examples of common letter symbols used to denote various circuit components are given in Table 1-5.

## Table 1-5 Examples of Circuit Component Letter Symbols

| Part | Letter | Example |
|------|--------|---------|
| Resistor | R | $R_3$, 120 kΩ |
| Capacitor | C | $C_5$, 20 pF |
| Inductor | L | $L_1$, 25 mH |
| Rectifier (metallic or crystal) | CR | $CR_2$ |
| Transformer | T | $T_2$ |
| Transistor | Q | $Q_5$, 2N482 Detector |
| Tube | V | $V_3$, 6AU6 1st IF amp |
| Jack | J | $J_1$ |

A schematic diagram of a two-transistor radio is shown in Figure 1-8. With the use of the diagram, it is possible to trace the operation of the circuit from the input signal at the antenna to the output signal at the headphones.

Note that subscripts are used to distinguish between various resistors, capacitors, etc.

Also note that the schematic diagram does not show the physical location of the components.

Another useful graphical tool is the block diagram.

The *block diagram* is used to show the relationship between the various component groups or stages in the operation of a circuit.

Figure 1-9 shows an example of a block diagram describing the signal path of a radio circuit. The block diagram gives no information about the specific components or wiring connections. It is of limited use but does give a simple way of illustrating the features of the circuit.

| | | | |
|---|---|---|---|
| Ammeter | —(A)— | Motor (dc) | —(M)— |
| Antenna | | Resistor (Fixed) | |
| Battery cell | | Resistor (variable) | |
| Battery | | Rheostat | |
| Capacitor (Fixed) | | | |
| Capacitor (variable) | | Switch | |
| Crystal | | Semiconductor diode | |
| Fuse | | Transformer (general) | |
| Generator (ac) | | Transformer (general) | |
| Generator (dc) | | Transistor (PNP) | |
| Ground | or | | |
| Inductor (air-core) | | Voltmeter | —(V)— |
| Inductor (iron-core) | | Wattmeter | —(W)— |
| Lamp | | Wires (connected) | |
| Motor (ac) | | Wires (unconnected) | |

**Figure 1-7** Standard Circuit Symbols

**Figure 1-8** Schematic of a two-transistor radio

**Figure 1-9** Block diagram of a radio receiver circuit

## Ohm's Law and Power

The practical electric circuit has at least four parts: (1) a source of electromotive force (emf), (2) conductors, (3) a load, and (4) a means of control (Figure 1-10). The source of the emf is commonly a battery or generator. The conductors are wires which offer low resistance to a current. The load resistor represents any device that uses electric energy. Control devices might be switches or protection devices such as fuses, circuit breakers, etc.

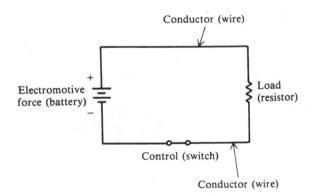

**Figure 1-10** Closed circuit

A ground symbol is often used to show that a number of wires are connected to a common point in a circuit. For example, in Figure 1-11($a$), the conductors are shown making a complete circuit. In Figure 1-11($b$), the same circuit is shown with two ground symbols $G1$ and $G2$. Electrically, the two schematics represent the same circuit.

## Important

A complete or *closed circuit* is an unbroken path for current, from the emf source, to flow through the load and return back to the source.

The circuit is an *open circuit* if there is not a closed path for the current to return to the source.

(*a*)        (*b*)

**Figure 1-11** Closed circuits (*a*) and (*b*) are the same

Resistance is the opposition to current flow.

A *resistor* is a device whose opposition to current flow is a known, specified value.

Resistance is measured in ohms ($\Omega$). See Figure 1-7 for the schematic symbols for resistors. **Fixed resistors** are designed to have a single value of resistance to a specified tolerance. The two main types of fixed resistors are carbon-composition and wire-wound. Variable resistors are called **potentiometers** or **rheostats**.

*Ohm's law* defines the relationship between current, voltage, and resistance. There are three ways to express Ohm's law mathematically.

1) The current in a circuit is equal to the voltage applied to the circuit divided by the resistance of the circuit:

$$I = \frac{V}{R}$$

(1-1)

2) The resistance of a circuit is equal to the voltage applied to the circuit divided by the current in the circuit:

$$R = \frac{V}{I}$$

(1-2)

3) The applied voltage to a circuit is equal to the product of the current and the resistance of the circuit:

$$V = I \times R$$

(1-3)

where $I$ = current, A , $R$ = resistance , $\Omega$ , and $V$ = voltage, V . If you know any two of the quantities $V$, $I$ and $R$, you can calculate the third.

**Example 1.2** An electric light bulb draws 1.0 A when operating on a 120-V dc circuit. What is the resistance of the bulb?

**Solution:** The first step is to sketch a schematic diagram, labeling the parts and showing the known values (Figure 1-12).

**Figure 1-12** Schematic for Example 1.2

Since $I$ and $V$ are known, we use (1-2) to solve for $R$

$$R = \frac{V}{I} = \frac{120}{1} = 120 \ \Omega$$

The *electric power* used in any part of the circuit is equal to the current $I$ in that part multiplied by the voltage $V$ across that part of the circuit

$$P = VI \tag{1-4}$$

The units of power are watts (W). Ohm's laws may be used to derive other useful forms of (1-4). Using (1-3),

$$P = VI = (IR)I = I^2 R \tag{1-5}$$

Using (1-1),

$$P = VI = V\left(\frac{V}{R}\right) = \frac{V^2}{R} \tag{1-6}$$

**Example 1.3** If the voltage across a 25 000 ohm (25 kΩ) resistor is 500 V, what is the power dissipated in the resistor?

**Solution:** Since $R$ and $V$ are known, use (1-6) to find $P$.

$$P = \frac{V^2}{R} = \frac{(500)^2}{25000} = 10 \text{ W}$$

⭐ **Note!**

A *motor* is a device which converts electric power into the mechanical power of a rotating shaft.

The electric power supplied to a motor is measured in watts; the mechanical power by a motor is measured in horsepower (hp). One horsepower is equivalent to 746 W of electric power.

Energy and work are expressed in identical units. Power is the rate of doing work. The joule (J) is the basic practical unit of work or energy. One watt is one joule per second. The kilowatthour (kWh) is a unit commonly used for large amounts of electric energy or work. The amount of kWh is just the product $kWh = kW \times h$ .

# Magnetism and Magnetic Fields

Most electrical equipment depends directly or indirectly upon magnetism. Magnetite (an iron ore) is a material which exhibits the phenomenon of magnetism and is called a *natural magnet*. The earth itself is a natural magnet. All other magnets that are human-made are called *artificial* magnets.

Every *magnet* has two points called *poles*: **north and south**. Much like electric charges, like magnetic poles repel each other and unlike poles attract each other.

Magnets impart a force on magnetic materials such as iron due to the *magnetic field*. The invisible force can be shown to exist by sprinkling small iron filings on a sheet of glass or paper over a bar magnet (Figure 1-13(*a*)). If the sheet is tapped gently, the filings will move into a definite pattern which describes the field of force around the magnet. The field seems to be made of **lines of force** that leave the north pole, travel through the air around the magnet, and continue through the magnet to the south pole to form a **closed loop** of force. The field is shown as lines of force (without filings) in Figure 1-13(*b*).

The entire group of magnetic field lines, which flow outward from the north pole of the magnet are called the *magnetic flux*.

The symbol for magnetic flux is the Greek letter phi $(\phi)$ . The SI unit for magnetic flux is the weber (Wb). One weber equals $1 \times 10^8$ magnetic field lines.

(a) Field outlined by iron filings

(b) Field indicated by lines of force

**Figure 1-13** Magnetic field of force around a bar magnet

The *magnetic flux density* is the magnetic flux per unit area of a section perpendicular to the direction of flux.

The symbol for magnetic flux density is $B$. The SI unit for magnetic flux density is webers per square meter (Wb/m$^2$). One weber per square meter is also called a **tesla** (T). The equation for magnetic flux density is

$$B = \frac{\phi}{A}$$

(1-7)

where $A$ is the area in m$^2$.

**Example 1.4** What is the flux density in teslas when there exists a flux of 600 $\mu$Wb through an area of 0.0003 m$^2$ ?

**Solution:** Substituting the values of $\phi$ and $A$ into (1-7) gives

$$B = \frac{\phi}{A} = \frac{6 \times 10^{-4} \text{ Wb}}{3 \times 10^{-4} \text{ m}^2} = 2 \text{ T}$$

Magnetic materials are those which are attracted or repelled by a magnet and which can be magnetized themselves. Iron and steel are the most common magnetic materials.

*Permeability* refers to the ability of a magnetic material to concentrate magnetic flux.

Any material that is easily magnetized has high permeability. A measure of permeability for different materials in comparison with air or vacuum is called **relative permeability**. The symbol for relative permeability is $\mu_r$. Classification of materials in terms of being magnetic or nonmagnetic generally includes three groups:

*1)* *Ferromagnetic materials*. These include iron, steel, nickel, cobalt and commercial alloys such as alnico and Permalloy. They can have values of $\mu_r$ in the thousands.

*2)* *Paramagnetic materials*. These include aluminum, platinum, manganese and chromium. Relative permeability is slightly greater than 1.

*3)* *Diamagnetic materials*. These include bismuth, antimony, copper, zinc, mercury, gold, and silver. Relative permeability is less than 1.

The value of permeability of air or a vacuum is $\mu_0 = 4\pi \times 10^{-7}$ H/m (henries/meter). The value of permeability for other materials is then $\mu = \mu_r \mu_0$ .

Electric current is another source of magnetic fields. Current flowing through a wire will produce concentric rings of magnetic force lines surrounding a wire. The strength of the magnetic field is proportional to the amplitude of the current (Figure 1-14).

High current                                    Low current

**Figure 1-14** Strength of magnetic field depends on current amplitude

The *right-hand rule* is used to determine the relationship between the flow of current in a conductor and the direction of the magnetic lines of force around the conductor. The thumb points in the direction of current flow and the fingers will curl in the direction of the lines of force (Figure 1-15). Current flow is from the positive side of the voltage source, through the coil, and back to the negative terminal.

Thumb points in
direction of current flow

Fingers curl in direction
of magnetic field

**Figure 1-15** Right-hand rule

Bending a straight wire into a loop produces a more dense set of magnetic field lines inside the loop. A coil of wire conductor is formed when there is more than one loop. To determine the polarity of the coil, use an alternate right-hand rule (Figure 1-16). The fingers curl in the direction of current flow. Adding an iron core inside the coil increases the flux density. The polarity of the core is the same as that of the coil.

The product of the current times the number of turns of the coil, which is expressed in *ampere-turns* (At), is know as the *magnetomotive force (mmf)*. If a coil with a certain number of ampere-turns is stretched out to twice its original length, the intensity of the magnetic field, that is, the concentration of the lines of force, will be half as great. The field intensity thus depends on how long the coil is. Expressed as an equation,

$$H = \frac{NI}{l}$$

where $H$ is the magnetic field intensity (At/m), $NI$ is the ampere-turns and $l$ is the length of the coil in m. This equation is for a solenoid. $H$ is the intensity at the center of the coil with an air core. With an iron core, $H$ is the intensity through the entire core and $l$ is the length between the poles of the iron core.

**Figure 1-16** Right-hand rule to find north pole of an electromagnet

# Electromagnetic Induction

In 1831, Michael Faraday discovered the principle of *electromagnetic induction*. It states that:

If a conductor "cuts across" lines of magnetic force, or if lines of force cut across a conductor, then an emf, or voltage, is induced across the ends of the conductor.

Consider a magnet with its lines of force concentrated only between the poles (Figure 1-17). A conductor $C$ which can be moved between the poles, is connected to a galvanometer $G$ used to indicate the presence of an emf:

- When the conductor is stationary, the galvanometer shows zero emf.

- If the conductor is moving outside the magnetic field at position 1, the reading is still zero.

**Figure 1-17** Demonstrating electromagnetic induction

- If the wire is moved to the left to position 2, it cuts the lines of magnetic force and $G$ will deflect to $A$.

- At position 3, $G$ swings back to zero as no lines are being cut.

- Move the conductor back through position 2 and the galvanometer $G$ will swing to $B$ indicating that an emf was induced but in the *opposite* direction.

- If the wire is held stationary at position 2, the reading will again read zero as there are no force lines being cut if it is not moving.

- If the conductor is moved up or down *parallel* to the lines of force so none is cut, $G$ will again read zero.

A very important application of relative motion between conductor and magnetic field is made in electric generators.

The value of the induced voltage depends on the number of turns of a coil and how fast the conductor cuts the lines of force or flux. Either the conductor or the flux can move. The equation to calculate the value of the induced voltage is

$$v_{ind} = N \frac{\Delta \phi}{\Delta t}$$

(1-8)

where $v_{ind}$ is the induced voltage (V), $N$ is the number of turns in a coil and $\Delta \phi / \Delta t$ is the rate at which flux cuts across the conductor (Wb/s). This is a form of **Faraday's law** for induced voltage. From (1-8), it is seen that $v_{ind}$ is determined by three factors:

1. The more lines of force that cut across the conductor, the higher the value of induced voltage.
2. The more turns in a coil, the higher the induced voltage.
3. The faster the flux cuts a conductor or the conductor cuts the flux, the higher the induced voltage because more lines of force cut the conductor within a given period of time.

**Example 1.5** The flux of an electromagnet is 6 Wb. The flux increases uniformly to 12 Wb in a period of 2 s. Calculate the voltage induced in a coil that has 10 turns if the coil is stationary in the magnetic field.

**Solution:** Write down the known values:

$\Delta \phi$ = change in flux = 12 Wb – 6 Wb = 6 Wb

$\Delta t$ = change in time corresponding to the increase in flux = 2 s

Then,

$$\frac{\Delta\phi}{\Delta t} = \frac{6}{2} = 3 \text{ Wb/s}$$

For $N = 10$ turns, (1-8) gives

$$v_{\text{ind}} = N\,\frac{\Delta\phi}{\Delta t} = 10(3) = 30 \text{ V}$$

## You Need to Know ✔

The polarity of the induced voltage is determined by *Lenz's law*. The induced voltage has the polarity that *opposes* the change causing the induction.

When a current flows as a result of the induced voltage, this current sets up a magnetic field about the conductor such that this conductor magnetic field reacts with the external magnetic field, producing the induced voltage to oppose the change in the external magnetic field. If the external field increases, the conductor magnetic field of the induced current will be in the opposite direction. If the external field decreases, the conductor magnetic field will be in the same direction, thus sustaining the external field.

**Example 1.6** A permanent magnet is moved into a coil and causes an induced current to flow in the circuit (Figure 1-18(*a*)). Determine the polarity of the coil and the direction of the induced current.

**Solution:** By Lenz's law, the left end of the coil must be the N pole to oppose the motion of the magnet. Then the direction of the induced current can be determined by the right-hand rule. If the right thumb points to the left for the N pole, the fingers coil around the direction of the current (Figure 1-18(*b*)).

(a)                                                           (b)

**Figure 1-18** Illustration of Lenz's law

# IMPORTANT THINGS TO REMEMBER:

✓ If enough energy is applied, some of the outermost valence electrons will leave an atom as free electrons. It is the movement of free electrons that provides electric current in conductors.

✓ Objects with like charges repel each other. Objects with opposite charges attract each other.

✓ Direct current (dc) moves through a conductor in one direction only. Alternating current (ac) reverses polarity periodically.

✓ The schematic diagram is a shorthand way to represent an electric circuit.

✓ Ohm's law defines the relationship between current, voltage, and resistance in a given circuit component.

✓ The electric power used in any part of the circuit is the product of the voltage times the current.

✓ Like magnetic poles repel each other. Unlike magnetic poles attract each other.

✓ The entire group of magnetic field lines which flow outward from the N pole of the magnet are called the magnetic flux.

✓ Permeability refers to the ability of a magnetic material to concentrate magnetic flux.

✓ A right-hand rule is used to determine the relationship between the flow of current in a conductor and the direction of the magnetic field lines surrounding the conductor due to the current.

✓ An alternate right-hand rule is used to determine the magnetic polarity of a coil of wire with current flowing in the wire.

✓ If a conductor cuts across lines of magnetic force, or if lines of force cut across a conductor, an emf, or voltage, is induced across the ends of the conductor.

✓ The polarity of the induced voltage is determined by Lenz's law.

# Chapter 2
# DIRECT-CURRENT: SERIES AND PARALLEL CIRCUITS

IN THIS CHAPTER:

27

## Voltage, Current, and Resistance in Series Circuits

A *series circuit* is a circuit in which there is only one path for current to flow along. In the series circuit (Figure 2-1), the current $I$ is the same in all parts of the circuit.

**Figure 2-1** A series circuit

When resistances are connected in series, the total resistance in the circuit $R_T$ is

$$R_T = R_1 + R_2 + R_3$$

The total voltage across a series circuit is the sum of the voltages across each resistance of the circuit (see Figure 2-2)

$$V_T = V_1 + V_2 + V_3$$

Ohm's law may be applied to the entire series circuit or to the individual parts of the circuit. Referring to Figure 2-2, the voltages across the resistors are given by $V_1 = IR_1$, $V_2 = IR_2$, $V_3 = IR_3$ .

**Example 2.1** A 95-V battery is connected in series with three resistors: $R_1 = 20$ ohms, $R_2 = 50$ ohms, $R_3 = 120$ ohms (Fig's. 2-1, 2-2). Find the voltage across each resistor.

**Solution:** Find the total resistance $R_T$.

$$R_T = R_1 + R_2 + R_3 = 20 + 50 + 120 = 190 \, \Omega$$

Find the current $I$. Using Ohm's law, $V_T = IR_T$. Solving, we get

$$I = \frac{V_T}{R_T} = \frac{95}{190} = 0.5 \text{ A}$$

**Figure 2-2** Voltage drops for a series circuit

Now the voltage across each resistor is found using Ohm's Law:
$V_1 = IR_1 = 0.5(20) = 10$ V, $V_2 = IR_2 = 0.5(50) = 25$ V, $V_3 = IR_3 = 0.5(120) = 60$ V.

The voltages $V_1$, $V_2$, and $V_3$ are known as *voltage drops*.

## Polarity of Voltage Drops

When there is a voltage drop across a resistance, one end must be at a higher potential (positive) than the other end (negative).

The *polarity* of the voltage drop is defined by using the convention where the higher potential end is the one for which the current enters the resistor.

Current direction is through $R_1$ from point $A$ to $B$ (Figure 2-3). The +/– signs are assigned as shown to indicate the polarity. Similarly, point $C$ is more positive than point $D$.

**Example 2.2** Refer to Example 2.1. Ground the negative terminal of the $V=95$ V battery (Figure 2-4). Mark the voltage drops in the circuit. Find the voltages at points $A$, $B$, $C$, and $D$ with respect to ground.

**Solution:** The positive terminals are marked as the points where the current enters the resistors. The voltage at point $A$ is the voltage across the battery. Therefore, $V_A = +95$ V. There is a voltage drop of 10 V across $R_1$ so $V_B = 95 - 10 = +85$ V. There is a voltage drop of 25 V across $R_2$ so $V_C = 85 - 25 = +60$ V. There is a voltage drop of 60 V across $R_3$ so $V_D = 60 - 60 = 0$ V. $V_D$ should be zero as it is the voltage of the ground.

**Figure 2-3** Polarity of voltage drops

**Figure 2-4** Example 2.2

# Conductors

A *conductor* is a material having many mobile electrons available for current flow.

Copper is the most common material used in electrical conductors with aluminum being second. Conductors have very low resistance. The function of conducting wires is to connect source voltages to resistances with minimal *IR* voltage drop in the conductor. Table 2-1 lists some standard wire sizes which correspond to the American Wire Gauge (AWG).

**Table 2-1 Copper Wire Table**

| Gauge No. | Diameter, $d$, mils | Circular-mil Area, $d^2$ | Ohms per 1000 ft of copper wire @ 25°C |
|-----------|---------------------|--------------------------|----------------------------------------|
| 6         | 162.0               | 26,250                   | 0.4028                                 |
| 12        | 80.81               | 6,530                    | 1.619                                  |
| 14        | 64.08               | 4,107                    | 2.575                                  |
| 16        | 50.82               | 2,583                    | 4.094                                  |
| 20        | 31.96               | 1,022                    | 10.35                                  |
| 28        | 12.64               | 159.8                    | 66.17                                  |

The cross-sectional area is measured in circular mils (cmil or CM). A mil is 0.001 inch. The number of circular mils in any circular area is cmil = CM = $d^2$. Note the following: As the gauge numbers increase, the wire sizes decrease and the resistance of the wires increase. To prevent wires from touching other circuit elements and short-circuiting, they are typically coated with an insulating material.

For any conductor, the resistance $R$ of a given length depends upon the length of the wire and the cross-sectional area of the wire according to the formula

$$R = \rho \frac{l}{A}$$

(2-1)

where $l$ is the length of the wire, $A$ is the cross-sectional area in CM, and $r$ is the resistivity in CM·ohms/ft. Table 2-2 lists some $R$ values for different metals of cross-sectional area of 1 CM.

**Table 2-2. Properties of Conducting Materials**

| Material | $\rho$ at 20°C, CM·ohms/ft |
|----------|---------------------------|
| Aluminum | 17 |
| Copper | 10.4 |
| Gold | 14 |
| Nickel | 52 |
| Silver | 9.8 |

**Example 2.3** What is the resistance of 500 ft of No. 20 copper wire?

**Solution:** From Table 2-1, the cross-sectional area of No. 20 wire is 1022 CM. From Table 2-2, $\rho$ = 10.4 CM·ohms/ft. Using (2-1),

$$R = \rho \frac{l}{A} = (10.4) \times \left( \frac{500}{1022} \right) = 5.09 \ \Omega$$

# Total Power in a Series Circuit

The total power $P_T$ in a series circuit is given by

$$P_T = I V_T \tag{2-2}$$

The total power $P_T$ produced by the source in a series circuit can also be expressed as a sum of the individual powers used in each part of the circuit

$$P_T = P_1 + P_2 + \ldots + P_n = IV_1 + IV_2 + \ldots + IV_n \tag{2-3}$$

**Example 2.4** In the circuit shown (Figure 2-5), find the total power $P_T$ dissipated by $R_1$ and $R_2$.

**Figure 2-5** Example 2.4

**Solution:** Find $I$ by Ohm's law.

$$I = \frac{V_T}{R_T} = \frac{V_T}{R_1 + R_2} = \frac{60}{5 + 10} = 4 \text{ A}$$

Find the power used in $R_1$ and $R_2$.

$$P_1 = I^2 R_1 = 4^2(5) = 80 \text{ W}$$

$$P_2 = I^2 R_2 = 4^2(10) = 160 \text{ W}$$

Find the total power using (2-3) by adding $P_1$ and $P_2$.

$$P_T = P_1 + P_2 = 80 + 160 = 240 \text{ W}$$

To compute the $P_T$ directly, use (2-2) and get $P_T = 4(60) = 240$ W.

# Voltage Drop by Proportional Parts

In a series circuit, each resistance $R$ provides a voltage drop $V$ equal to its proportional part of the applied voltage relative to the total resistance $R_T$.

Stated as an equation,

$$V = \frac{R}{R_T} V_T$$

(2-4)

**Example 2.5** Find the voltage drop across each resistor for the given circuit (Figure 2-6).

**Figure 2-6** Example 2.5

**Solution:** The total resistance $R_T$ is

$$R_T = R_1 + R_2 + R_3 = 20 + 30 + 50 = 100 \text{ k}\Omega$$

The individual voltages are found by substituting $R_1$, $R_2$, and $R_3$ into (2-4) giving

$$V_1 = \frac{20}{100}100 = 20 \text{ V}, \quad V_2 = \frac{30}{100}100 = 30 \text{ V}, \quad V_3 = \frac{50}{100}100 = 50 \text{ V}$$

# Voltage, Current and Resistance in Parallel Circuits

A *parallel circuit* is a circuit in which two or more components are connected across the same voltage source (Figure 2-7).

The resistors $R_1$, $R_2$, and $R_3$ are in parallel with each other and with the battery.

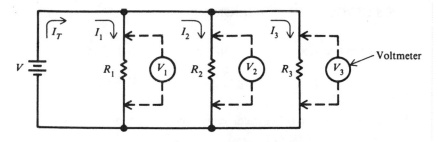

**Figure 2-7** A parallel circuit

Each parallel path is then a *branch* with its own current. The voltage across each parallel resistor is the same ($V = V_1 = V_2 = V_3$). Using Ohm's law, the total current $I_T$ is

$$I_T = I_1 + I_2 + I_3 = \frac{V}{R_1} + \frac{V}{R_2} + \frac{V}{R_3} \qquad (2\text{-}5)$$

**Example 2.6** For the given parallel circuit (Figure 2-8), what is the total current $I_T$?

**Figure 2-8** Example 2.6

**Solution:** Using Ohm's law,

$$I_1 = \frac{V}{R_1} = \frac{120}{15} = 8 \text{ A}, \quad I_2 = \frac{V}{R_2} = \frac{120}{15} = 8 \text{ A}, \quad I_3 = \frac{V}{R_3} = \frac{120}{12} = 10 \text{ A}$$

Then, from (2-5), $I_T = 8 + 8 + 10 = 26$ A.

# Resistances in Parallel

The total or equivalent resistance in a parallel circuit is given by

$$R_T = \frac{V}{I_T}$$

**Example 2.7** What is the total resistance for the parallel circuit in Example 2.6 (Figure 2-8)?

**Solution:** Using the results from Example 2.6,

$$R_T = \frac{V}{I_T} = \frac{120}{26} = 4.62 \ \Omega$$

## General Reciprocal Formula

The total parallel resistance for $n$ resistors is given by

$$\frac{1}{R_T} = \frac{1}{R_1} + \frac{1}{R_2} + \frac{1}{R_3} + \cdots + \frac{1}{R_n}$$

(2-6)

where $R_1, R_2, ..., R_n$ are the branch resistances.

**Example 2.8** Find the total resistance for the parallel circuit in Example 2.6 (Figure 2-8) using (2-6).

**Solution:** The branch resistances are given in Figure 2-8. Using (2-6),

$$\frac{1}{R_T} = \frac{1}{15} + \frac{1}{15} + \frac{1}{12} = 0.2167 \quad \Rightarrow \quad R_T = \frac{1}{0.2167} = 4.62 \ \Omega$$

## Simplified Formulas

The total resistance of equal resistors in parallel is equal to one resistor divided by the number of resistors

$$R_T = \frac{R}{N}$$

(2-7)

where $R$ is the branch resistance and $N$ is the number of parallel branches.

For two different resistors in parallel, the total resistance is given by

$$R_T = \frac{R_1 R_2}{R_1 + R_2}$$

(2-8)

**Example 2.9** What is the total resistance of a 6 ohm and an 18 ohm resistor in parallel?

**Solution:** Using (2-8),

$$R_T = \frac{R_1 R_2}{R_1 + R_2} = \frac{6(18)}{6 + 18} = \frac{108}{24} = 4.5 \, \Omega$$

## Note!

An *open circuit* is one in which the resistance in a branch is extremely high, ideally infinite ohms resistance. This means no current flows in the branch.

In Figure 2-9, the "x" indicates an open circuit in branch 2. No current will flow through branch 2 but current will flow through branches 1 and 3 if they are attached to a voltage source.

A *short circuit* is one in which the resistance in the branch is very low, ideally zero ohms resistance. Very high currents can flow in a short circuit.

In Figure 2-10, the solid line between points $a$ and $b$ indicate the presence of a short circuit. If a voltage source is applied between those points, no current will flow through the resistors $R_1$, $R_2$, or $R_3$ as the

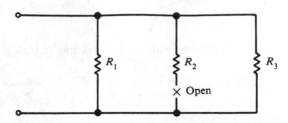

**Figure 2-9** Open circuit in a parallel branch

**Figure 2-10** Short in parallel circuit

voltage drop across a short circuit is zero (by Ohm's law). However, the current through the short circuit is very large, ideally approaching infinity in this example.

## Current Division in a Parallel Circuit

When only two branches are involved, the current in one branch will be some fraction of the total current $I_T$.

This fraction is the quotient of the second resistance divided by the sum of the resistances.

$$I_1 = \frac{R_2}{R_1 + R_2} I_T \; , \; I_2 = \frac{R_1}{R_1 + R_2} I_T$$

(2-9)

**Example 2.10** Find the branch currents $I_1$ and $I_2$ for the circuit shown in Figure 2-11. $I_T$ is 18 A and $R_1 = 3$ ohms and $R_2 = 6$ ohms.

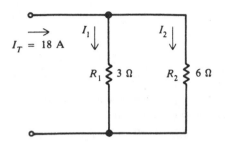

**Figure 2-11** Finding unknown branch currents

**Solution:** Using (2-9),

$$I_1 = \frac{6}{3+6} 18 = 12\text{ A}, \quad I_2 = \frac{3}{3+6} 18 = 6\text{ A}$$

# You Need to Know ✔

*Conductance* is the inverse of resistance. The symbol for conductance is $G$ and the units are Siemens (S).

For a resistor,

$$G = \frac{1}{R}$$

(2-10)

For example, a 6 ohm resistance has 1/6 S conductance. Using (2-6), the total conductance of parallel resistances is

$$G_T = G_1 + G_2 + \cdots + G_n = \frac{1}{R_1} + \frac{1}{R_2} + \ldots \frac{1}{R_n}$$

## Power in Parallel Circuits

The total power dissipated by parallel resistances equals the sum of the powers dissipated in each branch

$$P_T = P_1 + P_2 + \cdots + P_n$$

**Example 2.11** Find the power dissipated in each branch and the total power for the circuit in Figure 2-12.

**Figure 2-12** Example 2.11, power dissipation

**Solution:** The currents in the branches are

$$I_1 = \frac{V}{R_1} = 2 \text{ A}, \quad I_2 = \frac{V}{R_2} = 4 \text{ A}$$

The power in each branch is
$P_1 = VI_1 = 20(2) = 40 \text{ W}, P_2 = VI_2 = 20(4) = 80 \text{ W}$
The total power is $P_T = 40+80 = 120$ W.

# IMPORTANT THINGS TO REMEMBER:

✓ The total resistance $R_T$ of a series circuit is the sum of the individual resistances.

✓ The polarity is assigned as positive for the point where the current enters the resistor and negative where the current exits.

✓ As the gauge numbers increase, the wire sizes decrease and the resistance of the wires increase.

✓ The total power $P_T$ produced by the source in a series circuit can also be expressed as a sum of the individual powers used in each part of the circuit.

✓ The voltage drop across a series resistor $R$ is a fraction of the total voltage $V_T$. The fraction of $V_T$ is the ratio of $R$ to the total resistance $R_T$.

✓ The total current in a parallel circuit is the sum of the branch currents (2-5).

✓ Resistances in parallel can be computed using the reciprocal formula (2-6).

✓ For $n$ identical resistors $R$, the total resistance is $R/n$.

✓ For two resistors $R_1$ and $R_2$, the total parallel resistance is the product $R_1 R_2$ over the sum $R_1 + R_2$.

✓ An open circuit is a branch through which no current can flow.

✓ A short circuit is a branch through which very large current can flow. There is no voltage drop across a short circuit.

✓ Conductance is the inverse of resistance (2-10).

## Solved Problems

**Solved Problem 2.1** Find $I$, $V_1$, $V_2$, $P_2$, and $R_2$ for the circuit shown in Figure 2-13.

**Figure 2-13** Circuit for Solved Problem 2.1

**Step 1:** Find $I$. Use the power formula $P_1 = I^2 R_1$ to get

$$I = \sqrt{\frac{P_1}{R_1}} = \sqrt{\frac{80}{5}} = \sqrt{16} = 4 \text{ A}$$

**Step 2:** Find $V_1$, $V_2$

$$V_1 = IR_1 = 4(5) = 20 \text{ V}$$

$$V_2 = V_T - V_1 = 120 - 20 = 100 \text{ V}$$

**Step 3:** Find $P_2$, $R_2$

$$P_2 = V_2 I = 100(4) = 400 \text{ W}$$

$$R_2 = \frac{V_2}{I} = \frac{100}{4} = 25 \text{ } \Omega$$

**Solved Problem 2.2:** For the circuit in Figure 2-14, find (*a*) each branch current; (*b*) $I_T$; (*c*) $R_T$; (*d*) $P_1$, $P_2$, $P_3$, and $P_T$

**Figure 2-14** Circuit for Solved Problem 2.2

**Step 1:** Using Ohm's law,

$$I_1 = \frac{V_T}{R_1} = \frac{120}{4000} = 0.03 \text{ A} = 30 \text{ mA}$$

$$I_2 = \frac{V_T}{R_2} = \frac{120}{8200} = 0.0146 \text{ A} = 14.6 \text{ mA}$$

$$I_3 = \frac{V_T}{R_3} = \frac{120}{2000} = 0.06 \text{ A} = 60 \text{ mA}$$

$$I_T = I_1 + I_2 + I_3 = 30 + 14.6 + 60 = 104.6 \text{ mA}$$

$$R_T = \frac{V_T}{I_T} = \frac{120}{.1046} = 1147 \ \Omega = 1.15 \text{ k}\Omega$$

**Step 2:** Using the power formula $P = I^2 R$,

$$P_1 = I_1^2 R_1 = (0.03)^2 (4000) = 3.60 \text{ W}$$

$$P_2 = I_2^2 R_2 = (0.0146)^2 (8200) = 1.75 \text{ W}$$

$$P_3 = I_3^2 R_3 = (0.06)^2 (2000) = 7.20 \text{ W}$$

$$P_T = I_T^2 R_T = P_1 + P_2 + P_3 = 3.60 + 1.75 + 7.20 = 12.6 \text{ W}$$

# Chapter 3
# KIRCHHOFF'S LAWS AND NETWORK CALCULATIONS

## Kirchhoff's Voltage Law (KVL)

*Kirchhoff's voltage law (KVL)* states that *the voltage applied to a closed circuit equals the sum of the voltage drops in that circuit* and is given by

$$V_A = V_1 + V_2 + V_3$$

Another way of stating KVL is that the algebraic sum of the voltage rises and voltage drops around a closed circuit must be equal to zero. A voltage source is considered to be a rise and the voltage across a resistor is considered a voltage drop. The algebraic sum can be written as

$$\sum V = V_A - V_1 - V_2 - V_3 = 0$$

(3-1)

We assign a "+" sign to a voltage rise and a "−" sign to a drop. Equation (3-1) is valid for any closed loop. Consider the circuit in Figure 3-1.

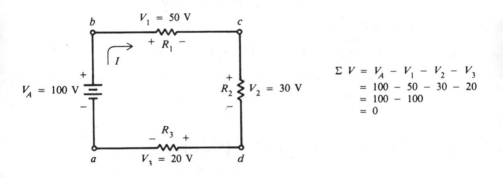

$$\begin{aligned} \Sigma V &= V_A - V_1 - V_2 - V_3 \\ &= 100 - 50 - 30 - 20 \\ &= 100 - 100 \\ &= 0 \end{aligned}$$

**Figure 3-1** Illustration of $\Sigma V = 0$

Going around loop *abcda*, we go through voltage rise $V_A = 100$ V and voltage drops $V_1 = 50$ V, $V_2 = 30$ V and $V_3 = 20$ V. Note that when going around the loop, voltage rises are noted for directions going from the "−" sign to the "+" sign while drops go from the "+" sign to the "−" sign.

**Example 3.1** Determine the voltage $V_B$ (Figure 3-2).

**Figure 3-2** Finding a source voltage

**Solution:** The direction of current flow is shown by the arrow. Using (3-1),

$$\sum V = V_A - V_1 - V_2 - V_B - V_3 = 0$$

Solving for $V_B$,

$$V_B = V_A - V_1 - V_2 - V_3 = 15 - 3 - 6 - 2 = 4 \text{ V}$$

Since $V_B$ was found to be positive, the assumed direction of current is in fact the direction of current flow.

# Kirchhoff's Current Law (KCL)

*Kirchhoff's current law (KCL)* states that *the sum of the currents entering a node (junction) is equal to the sum of currents leaving the node.* In other words, the sum of all currents at a node must equal zero.

In Figure 3-3, there are six currents entering or leaving the node. Assigning "+" signs for currents entering the node and "–"signs for those leaving the nodes, Kirchhoff's current law can be stated as

$$\sum I = I_1 - I_2 + I_3 + I_4 - I_5 + I_6 = 0$$

(3-2)

**Example 3.2** Find the unknown current at node $P$ in Figure 3-4.

**Solution:** The algebraic sum of all currents at node $P$ is zero per (3-2).

$$\sum I = I_1 + I_2 - I_3 + I_4 = 0$$

Solving for $I_4$,

$$I_4 = -I_1 - I_2 + I_3 = -1\,\text{A}$$

Common point, junction, or node

**Figure 3-3** Currents at a common point or node

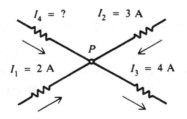

**Figure 3-4** Finding the unknown current

## Mesh Analysis

A simplification of Kirchhoff's laws is a method that makes use of *mesh* or *loop* currents. A mesh is any closed circuit path (loop).

Then we assign a mesh current to each mesh. The direction is arbitrary but clockwise is a commonly used direction. KVL is then applied around each mesh and the unknown mesh currents are then determined. Once the currents are known, the voltage for any resistor can be found.

Consider the circuit in Figure 3-5. There are two meshes in the circuit. Mesh 1 is *abcda* and mesh 2 is *adefa*. To find the unknown mesh currents $I_1$ and $I_2$, follow these steps:

**Figure 3-5** Finding mesh currents and voltage drops

**Step 1:** The mesh currents are assumed in the clockwise direction. The voltage polarities are marked across each resistor, consistent with each assumed current (the positive polarity is assigned to the node where the current enters).

**Step 2:** Apply KVL to each mesh in the direction of the assumed current flow. Note that both currents flow in $R_2$ and that is why it has two sets of polarities assigned. Tracing mesh 1 in the *abcda* direction,

$$V_A - I_1 R_1 - I_1 R_2 + I_2 R_2 = 0$$

Factoring to get known voltage $V_A$ on the right-hand side,

$$+ I_1 (R_1 + R_2) - I_2 R_2 = V_A \qquad (3\text{-}3)$$

Tracing mesh 2 in the *adefa* direction,

$$-I_2 R_2 + I_1 R_2 - I_2 R_3 - V_B = 0$$

Factoring to get known voltage $V_B$ on the right-hand side,

$$+I_1 R_2 - I_2 (R_2 + R_3) = V_B \qquad (3\text{-}4)$$

**Step 3:** Find $I_1$ and $I_2$ by solving Eqs. (3-3) and (3-4) simultaneously.

**Example 3.3** Given $V_A = 58$ V, $V_B = 10$ V, $R_1 = 4$ ohms, $R_2 = 3$ ohms, and $R_3 = 2$ ohms (Figure 3-5), find all mesh currents and voltage drops in the circuit.

**Solution:** The mesh currents are shown in Figure 3-5. The direction and polarity of voltage drops are assigned per Step 1 above. Applying KVL, and substituting into (3-3) and (3-4),

$$+I_1(R_1 + R_2) - I_2 R_2 = +I_1(4+3) - I_2(3) = 7I_1 - 3I_2 = 58$$

$$+I_1(R_2) - I_2(R_2 + R_3) = +I_1(3) - I_2(3+2) = 3I_1 - 5I_2 = 10$$

Solving the equations simultaneously gives $I_1 = 10$ A and $I_2 = 4$ A. The voltage drops are then found using Ohm's law:

$$V_1 = I_1 R_1 = 10(4) = 40 \text{ V}$$

$$V_2 = (I_1 - I_2)R_2 = (10 - 4)(3) = 18 \text{ V}$$

$$V_3 = I_2 R_3 = 4(2) = 8 \text{ V}$$

To check the solutions, you can check the solution around loop *abcdefa* using KVL:

$$\sum V = V_A - V_1 - V_3 - V_B = 58 - 40 - 8 - 10 = 0$$

which it should be per KVL from (3-1).

## Nodal Analysis

Another method for solving a circuit with mesh currents uses the voltage drops to specify the currents at a node. The node equations are written to satisfy Kirchhoff's current law.

A *principal node* has three or more connections.

Consider the circuit in Figure 3-6. The letters $A$, $B$, $G$, and $N$ label the nodes. $G$ and $N$ are principal nodes.

A *node voltage* is the voltage with respect to the *reference node*.

In Figure 3-6, node $G$ is the reference node, denoted by the ground symbol. For example, $V_N$ is the node voltage for node $N$.

**Figure 3-6** Node voltage analysis

KCL is used for all principal nodes with the exception of the reference node. The KCL analysis yields equations in terms of the unknown node voltages. Once node voltages are known, all voltages and currents can then be determined.

**Example 3.4** Find all voltage drops and currents for the circuit in Figure 3-6 using node voltage analysis.

**Solution:** The solution is presented in order of the required steps.

**Step 1:** Assign current directions and label the nodes (Figure 3-6). Mark the polarity of the voltage to be consistent with the assumed direction of the current.

**Step 2:** Apply KCL at the principal node $N$ and solve for $V_N$.

$$\sum I = 0 = I_1 + I_2 - I_3 \Rightarrow I_3 = I_1 + I_2$$

Using Ohm's law,

$$I_3 = \frac{V_N}{R_2} = \frac{V_A - V_N}{R_1} + \frac{V_B - V_N}{R_3}$$

$$\frac{V_N}{3} = \frac{58 - V_N}{4} + \frac{10 - V_N}{2}$$

Solving, $V_N = 18$ V.

**Step 3:** Solve for voltage drops and currents.

$$V_1 = V_A - V_N = 58 - 18 = 40 \text{ V}$$

$$V_2 = V_N = 18 \text{ V}$$

$$V_3 = V_B - V_N = 10 - 18 = -8 \text{ V}$$

$$I_1 = \frac{V_1}{R_1} = \frac{40}{4} = 10 \text{ A}$$

$$I_2 = \frac{V_3}{R_3} = \frac{-8}{2} = -4 \text{ A}$$

$$I_3 = \frac{V_2}{R_2} = \frac{18}{3} = 6 \text{ A}$$

The result can be checked using KCL:

$$I_3 = I_1 + I_2 = 10 - 4 = 6 \text{ A}$$

# Y and Delta Networks

The circuits in Figure 3-7 are called a T ("tee") or a Y ("wye") network due to their shape. The T and Y are essentially the same network with a different shape (both having three resistors connected to one node).

**Figure 3-7** Form of a T or a Y network

The circuits shown in Figure 3-8 are called a π ("pi") or a Δ ("delta") network. The π and Δ are essentially the same network with a different shape (both having three resistors connected through three nodes).

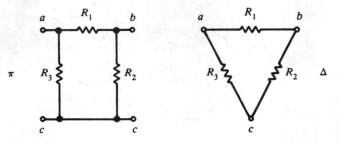

**Figure 3-8** Form of a π or Δ network

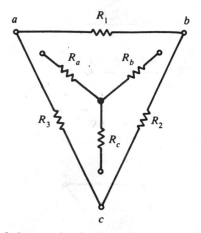

**Figure 3-9** Conversion between Y and Δ networks

It is often desirable to convert Y to Δ or Δ to Y to simplify the solution. The formulas for the conversions are derived using Kirchhoff's laws. Note that the resistances for the Y have subscript letters while the resistances in the Δ are numbered (Figure 3-9).

**Δ to Y Conversion:** Refer to Figure 3-9.

$$R_a = \frac{R_1 R_3}{R_1 + R_2 + R_3}$$

(3-5)

$$R_b = \frac{R_1 R_2}{R_1 + R_2 + R_3}$$

(3-6)

$$R_c = \frac{R_2 R_3}{R_1 + R_2 + R_3}$$

(3-7)

**Y to Δ Conversion:** Refer to Figure 3-9.

$$R_1 = \frac{R_a R_b + R_b R_c + R_c R_a}{R_c}$$

(3-8)

$$R_2 = \frac{R_a R_b + R_b R_c + R_c R_a}{R_a}$$

(3-9)

$$R_3 = \frac{R_a R_b + R_b R_c + R_c R_a}{R_b}$$

(3-10)

**Example 3.5** Use network conversions to find the equivalent total resistance $R_T$ between nodes $a$ and $d$ for the circuit in Figure 3-10.

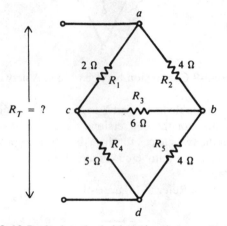

**Figure 3-10** Reducing the bridge circuit to equivalent $R_T$

**Solution:** Use the following steps:

**Step 1:** Transform $\Delta$ network $abc$ into its equivalent Y using (3-5,6,7).

$$R_a = \frac{2(4)}{2+4+6} = \frac{8}{12} = 0.667 \ \Omega, \ R_b = \frac{4(6)}{12} = 2 \ \Omega, \ R_c = \frac{2(6)}{12} = 1 \ \Omega$$

**Step 2:** Replace the $\Delta$ with its Y equivalent (Figure 3-11).

**Step 3:** Simplify the series-parallel circuit. First, combine the parallel branches $R_c + R_4 = 1 + 5 = 6 \ \Omega$ and $R_b + R_5 = 2 + 4 = 6 \ \Omega$ using (2-7)

$$R_p = \frac{6}{2} = 3 \ \Omega$$

Finally, the total resistance is

$$R_T = R_a + R_p = 0.667 + 3 = 3.667 \ \Omega$$

**Figure 3-11** Simplifying the circuit from Example 3.5

## Superposition

In order to superpose currents and voltages, all components must be linear and bilateral. *Linear* means that for a given component, the current is proportional to the applied voltage (i.e., Ohm's law is obeyed). *Bilateral* means that the current is the same amount for opposite polarities of the source voltage.

The ***superposition theorem*** states that *in a linear, bilateral network with two or more sources, the current or voltage for any component is the algebraic sum of the effects produced by each source acting independently.*

## Note!

In order to use one source at a time, all other sources are effectively removed from the circuit. A *voltage source is replaced by a short circuit* and a *current source is replaced by an open circuit.*

**Example 3.6** Find the branch currents $I_1$, $I_2$, and $I_3$ using superposition (Figure 3-12).

**Figure 3-12** Superposition applied to a two-mesh circuit

**Solution:** Use the following steps:

**Step 1:** Find the currents produced by $V_1$ only. Replace voltage source $V_2$ with a short circuit (Figure 3-13).

**Figure 3-13** Solution with $V_2$ replaced by a short circuit

Find current $I_{1,V1}$ using Figure 3-14. The equivalent series-parallel resistance $R_4$ is

$$R_4 = R_1 + \frac{R_2 R_3}{R_2 + R_3} = 1 + \frac{1(1)}{1+1} = 1.5 \ \Omega$$

$$I_{1,V1} = \frac{V_1}{R_4} = \frac{3}{1.5} = 2 \ \text{A}$$

**Figure 3-14** Finding $I_{1,V1}$

$I_{1,V1}$ will divide symmetrically because of the equal resistances $R_2$ and

$$I_{2,V1} = -\frac{1}{2} I_{1,V1} = -1 \ \text{A}$$

$R_3$ giving

$$I_{3,V1} = \frac{1}{2} I_{1,V1} = 1 \ \text{A}$$

**Step 2:** Find the currents produced by $V_2$ only. Replace $V_1$ with a short circuit (Figure 3-15).

$V_1$ is short-circuited

**Figure 3-15** Solution with $V_1$ replaced by a short circuit

Find current $I_{2,V2}$ using Figure 3-16. The equivalent series-parallel resistance $R_5$ is

$$R_5 = R_2 + \frac{R_1 R_3}{R_1 + R_3} = 1 + \frac{1(1)}{1+1} = 1.5 \ \Omega$$

$$I_{2,V2} = \frac{V_2}{R_5} = \frac{4.5}{1.5} = 3 \ \text{A}$$

**Figure 3-16** Finding $I_{2,V2}$

$I_{2,V2}$ will divide symmetrically because of the equal resistances $R_1$ and

$$I_{3,V2} = \frac{1}{2} I_{2,V2} = 1.5 \ \text{A}$$

$R_3$ giving

$$I_{1,V2} = -\frac{1}{2} I_{2,V2} = -1.5 \ \text{A}$$

**Step 3:** Superpose the two sets of currents to find the current produced by both $V_1$ and $V_2$:

$$I_1 = I_{1,V1} + I_{1,V2} = 2 - 1.5 = 0.5 \ \text{A}$$

$$I_2 = I_{2,V1} + I_{2,V2} = -1 + 3 = 2 \ \text{A}$$

$$I_3 = I_{3,V1} + I_{3,V2} = 1 + 1.5 = 2.5 \ \text{A}$$

## Thevenin's Theorem

***Thevenin's theorem*** states that *any linear network of voltage sources and resistances, if viewed from any two nodes in the network, can be replaced by an equivalent resistance $R_{Th}$ in series with an equivalent voltage source $V_{Th}$.*

$R_{Th}$ is the resistance looking into nodes $a$ and $b$ with all internal voltage sources replaced with short circuits (see Figure 3-17). $V_{Th}$ is the Thevenin voltage that would appear at nodes $a$ and $b$ if no load is attached. For this reason, the Thevenin voltage is also called the open-circuit voltage. Use of Thevenin's theorem greatly simplifies calcula-tions in many cases where the network is attached to changing external networks

(a)                                                        (b)

**Figure 3-17** Thevenin equivalent, $V_{Th}$, series $R_{Th}$

**Example 3.7** Find the Thevenin equivalent to the circuit at terminals $a$ and $b$. See Figure 3-18.

**Solution**

**Step 1:** Find $R_{Th}$. If the voltage source $V$ is replaced by a short circuit, the resistors $R_1$ and $R_2$ are in parallel giving

$$R_{Th} = \frac{R_1 R_2}{R_1 + R_2} = \frac{4(6)}{4 + 6} = 2.4 \ \Omega$$

**Figure 3-18** Finding the Thevenin equivalent

**Step 2:** Find $V_{Th}$. This is the same as the voltage drop across $R_2$. Using (2-4),

$$V_{Th} = V \frac{R_2}{R_1 + R_2} = 10 \frac{6}{4+6} = 6 \text{ V}$$

See Figure 3-19 for the equivalent circuit.

**Figure 3-19** Thevenin equivalent without load

## Norton's Theorem

Norton's theorem is used to simplify a network in terms of currents instead of voltages.

*Norton's theorem* states that *any network connected to terminals a and b (Figure 3-20) can be replaced by a single current source $I_N$ in parallel with a single resistance $R_N$.*

$R_N$ is the resistance looking into nodes *a* and *b* with all internal current sources replaced with open circuits and voltage sources replaced by

short circuits. The value of $R_N$ is the same as the Thevenin resistance $R_{Th.}$
$I_N$ is equal to the current through the *ab* terminals if a short-circuit is
attached. For this reason, the Norton current is also called the shortcircuit
current. Use of Norton's theorem greatly simplifies calculations in many
cases where the network is attached to changing external networks.

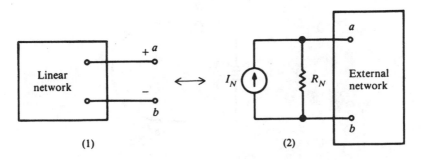

**Figure 3-20** Norton equivalent, $I_N$, and parallel $R_N$

**Example 3.8** Find the Norton equivalent to the circuit at terminals *a*
and *b*. See Figure 3-18.

**Solution:**

**Step 1:** Find $R_N$. If the voltage source $V$ is replaced with a short circuit,
the resistors $R_1$ and $R_2$ are in parallel giving

$$R_N = \frac{R_1 R_2}{R_1 + R_2} = \frac{4(6)}{4+6} = 2.4\ \Omega = R_{Th}$$

**Step 2:** Find $I_N$. Short terminals *ab*. The equivalent resistance of the
short circuit in parallel with the $6\ \Omega$ -resistor is just a short circuit (see
Figure 3-21).

The only resistance remaining in the circuit is $R_1$. Using Ohm's law, the
current in the short circuit is

$$I_N = \frac{V}{R_1} = \frac{10}{4} = 2.5 \text{ A}$$

The Norton equivalent circuit is shown in Figure 3-22.

**Figure 3-21** Circuit with terminals *ab* short circuited

**Figure 3-22** Norton equivalent circuit for Example 3.8

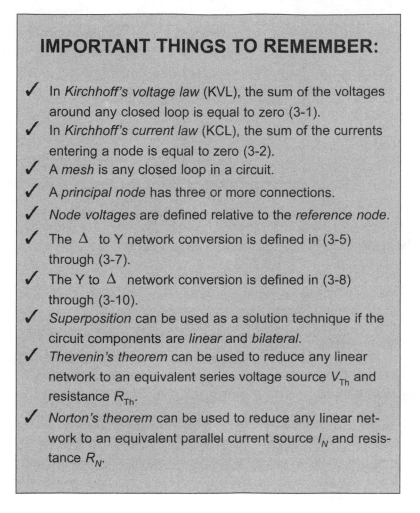

# IMPORTANT THINGS TO REMEMBER:

✓ In *Kirchhoff's voltage law* (KVL), the sum of the voltages around any closed loop is equal to zero (3-1).
✓ In *Kirchhoff's current law* (KCL), the sum of the currents entering a node is equal to zero (3-2).
✓ A *mesh* is any closed loop in a circuit.
✓ A *principal node* has three or more connections.
✓ *Node voltages* are defined relative to the *reference node*.
✓ The $\Delta$ to Y network conversion is defined in (3-5) through (3-7).
✓ The Y to $\Delta$ network conversion is defined in (3-8) through (3-10).
✓ *Superposition* can be used as a solution technique if the circuit components are *linear* and *bilateral*.
✓ *Thevenin's theorem* can be used to reduce any linear network to an equivalent series voltage source $V_{Th}$ and resistance $R_{Th}$.
✓ *Norton's theorem* can be used to reduce any linear network to an equivalent parallel current source $I_N$ and resistance $R_N$.

## Solved Problems

**Solved Problem 3.1** Find all mesh currents and voltage drops for the two-mesh circuit in Figure 3-23.

**Figure 3-23** Two-mesh circuit for Solved Problem 3.1

**Step 1:** Show the direction of mesh currents as indicated.

**Step 2:** Apply KVL for meshes 1 and 2:

$$110 - 5I_1 - 190 - 5I_1 + 5I_2 = 0$$

Mesh 1, *abcda*:
$$\Rightarrow -10I_1 + 5I_2 = 80 \tag{1}$$

$$5I_1 - 5I_2 + 190 - 15I_2 - 20I_2 = 0$$

Mesh 2, *adefa*:
$$\Rightarrow 5I_1 - 40I_2 = -190 \tag{2}$$

**Step 3:** Find $I_1$ and $I_2$ by solving (1) and (2) simultaneously

$$-10I_1 + 5I_2 = 80$$
$$5I_1 - 40I_2 = -190$$

Multiply (2) by 2 and add to get

$$-10I_1 + 5I_2 = 80$$
$$10I_1 - 80I_2 = -380$$

$$-75I_2 = -300$$

$$I_2 = \frac{300}{75} = 4 \text{ A}$$

Substitute $I_1 = 4$ A into (1) to get

$$-10I_1 + 5(4) = 80 \quad \Rightarrow \quad I_1 = -6 \text{ A}$$

The negative sign means the assumed direction for $I_1$ was not correct. $I_1$ is actually going in the counterclockwise direction. In branch $ad$, $I_1$ and $I_2$ are going in the same direction. Therefore,

$$I_{ad} = I_1 + I_2 = 4 + 6 = 10 \text{ A}$$

**Step 4:** Find the voltage drops.

$$V_1 = I_1 R_1 = 6(5) = 30 \text{ V}$$

$$V_2 = (I_1 + I_2)R_2 = 10(5) = 50 \text{ V}$$

$$V_3 = I_2 R_3 = 4(15) = 60 \text{ V}$$

$$V_4 = I_2 R_4 = 4(20) = 80 \text{ V}$$

**Step 5:** Check. Use KVL to trace the loop $abcdefa$ (use the original assumed direction for $I_1$ and $I_2$).

$$+V_A - I_1 R_1 - I_2 R_3 - I_2 R_4 = 0$$

$$+110 - (-6)(5) - 4(15) - 4(20) = 0$$

$$+110 + 30 - 60 - 80 = 0$$

$$+140 - 140 = 0 \quad \Rightarrow \quad \textit{Checks out!}$$

**Solved Problem 3.2** Find the voltage $V_2$ across $R_2$ by method of node-voltage analysis for the circuit in Figure 3-24.

**Figure 3-24** 3-node circuit for Solved Problem 3.2

**Step 1:** Assume direction of currents shown. Mark voltage polarities. Show nodes $A$, $B$, $N$, $G$.

**Step 2:** Apply KCL at principal node $N$.

$$I_3 = I_1 + I_2 \tag{1}$$

$$I_3 = \frac{V_2}{R_2} = \frac{V_N}{2} \tag{1a}$$

$$I_1 = \frac{V_1}{R_1} = \frac{V_A - V_N}{R_1} = \frac{12 - V_N}{8} \tag{1b}$$

$$I_2 = \frac{V_3}{R_3} = \frac{V_B - V_N}{R_3} = \frac{V_B - V_N}{4} \tag{1c}$$

We are unable to determine $V_B$ by inspection in (1c) because voltage drop $V_4$ is not given. So we use KVL to find $V_B$ by tracing the complete circuit from $G$ to $B$ in the direction of $I_2$ and back from $B$ to $G$ (voltage from $B$ to $G$ is $V_B$). This gives

$$-6 - 2I_2 - V_B = 0 \quad \Rightarrow \quad V_B = -6 - 2I_2 \tag{2}$$

Substituting (2) into (1c) gives

$$I_2 = \frac{-6 - 2I_2 - V_N}{4}$$

$$I_2 = \frac{-6 - V_N}{6}$$

Substituting the three expressions for current into (1) gives

$$\frac{V_N}{2} = \frac{12 - V_N}{8} + \frac{-6 - V_N}{6} \tag{3}$$

Now equation (3) has just the one unknown, $V_N$.

**Step 3:** Find $V_2$ $(V_2 = V_N)$. Multiply both sides of (3) by 24

$$12V_N = (36 - 3V_N) + (-24 - 4V_N)$$
$$19V_N = 12$$
$$V_2 = V_N = \frac{12}{19} = 0.632 \text{ V}$$

**Solved Problem 3.3** Find the Thevenin equivalents $V_{\text{Th}}$ and $R_{\text{Th}}$ for Figure 3-25.

**Figure 3-25** Circuit for Solved Problem 3.3

**Step 1:** Find $R_{\text{Th}}$ by replacing the $V$ with a short circuit. $R_{\text{Th}}$ is essentially the resistance looking into terminals $ab$ which is the $2 - \Omega$ resistor in parallel with the series $3+5=8\ \Omega$ resistance.

$$R_{Th} = \frac{2(8)}{2+8} = \frac{16}{10} = 1.6\ \Omega$$

**Step 2:** $V_{Th}$ is the drop across the $2-\Omega$ resistor.

$$V_{Th} = V\frac{R_2}{R_1+R_2+R_3} = 12\frac{2}{3+2+5} = 12\frac{2}{10} = 2.4\ V$$

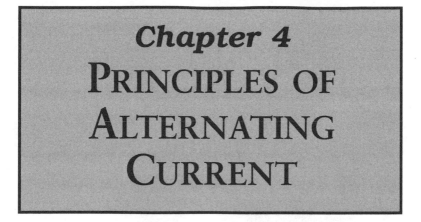

# Chapter 4
# PRINCIPLES OF ALTERNATING CURRENT

IN THIS CHAPTER:

✔ Generating an Alternating Voltage
✔ Sine Wave Basics
✔ Phasors
✔ Characteristic Values of Voltage, Current, and Power in AC Circuits
✔ Solved Problems

## Generating an Alternating Voltage

An *ac voltage* is one that continually changes in magnitude and periodically reverses polarity (Figure 4-1).

The voltages above the horizontal axis have positive (+) polarity, while the voltages below the horizontal axis have negative (–) polarity.

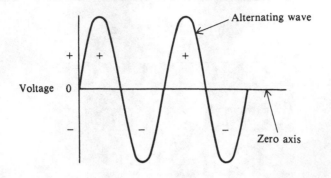

**Figure 4-1** An ac voltage waveform

An ac voltage can be produced by a generator, called an alternator.

In the simplified generator shown (Figure 4–2), the conductor loop rotates through the magnetic field and cuts lines of force to generate an induced ac voltage across its terminals. One complete revolution of the loop around the circle is a *cycle*. Figure 4-3 shows the output voltage versus angle of rotation of the loop. A cycle is the period between two successive repeated points. The loop starts at position *A* and completes the first cycle when it returns to that position. The cycle of voltage repeats again between positions *A'* to *A"*.

## Sine Wave Basics

The voltage waveform in Figure 4-3 is a *sine wave*.

The instantaneous value of voltage $v$ at any point on the sine wave is expressed by the equation $v = V_M \sin \theta$ where $V_M$ is the maximum value of voltage and $\theta$ is the angle of rotation (degrees or radians).

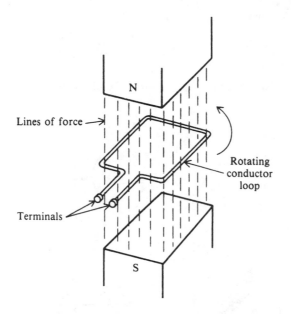

**Figure 4-2** Loop rotating in a magnetic field

## ⭐ Note!

When a sine wave of alternating voltage is connected across a load resistance, the current that flows in the circuit is also a sine wave.

**Example 4.1** An AC generator with $v = 10 \sin \theta$ V is applied across a load resistance of $10 \, \Omega$ (Figure 4-4(a)). Show the resulting alternating current.

**Solution:** The instantaneous value of current is $i = v/R$. In a pure resistance circuit, the current waveform follows the polarity of the voltage waveform. The maximum value of current is

$$I_M = \frac{V_M}{R} = \frac{10}{10} = 1 \text{ A}$$

In the form of an equation, $i = I_M \sin\theta$ . The plot is in Figure 4-4($b$).

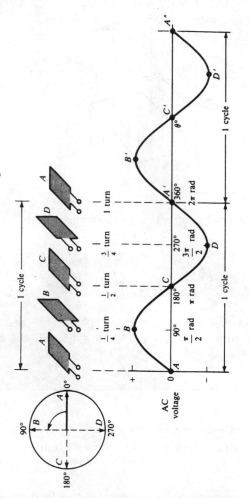

**Figure 4-3** Two cycles of alternating voltage generated by rotating loop. (*From B. Grob, Basic Electronics, 4th ed., McGraw-Hill, New York, 1977, p. 313*

**Figure 4-4** AC voltage applied to a resistive load

The number of cycles per second is called *frequency*. It is indicated by the symbol $f$ and is expressed in hertz (Hz). One cycle per second is one hertz.

The amount of time for the completion of one cycle is the *period*. It is indicated by the symbol $T$ for time and is expressed in seconds (s).

The frequency and period are related by

$$f = \frac{1}{T} \text{ or } T = \frac{1}{f}$$

The higher the frequency the shorter the period. The angle of 360° represents the angular variation for one period. Therefore, when plotting the sine waves, we can put the horizontal axis in time or angle.

**Example 4.2** An ac current has a period of $T = 1/100$ s. What is $f$?

**Solution:** The frequency is $f = 1/T = 100 \ Hz$. See Figure 4-5.

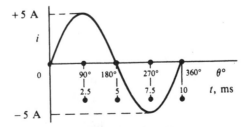

**Figure 4-5** Sinusoidal current for Example 4.2

The *wavelength* is the length of one complete wave or cycle. It is denoted by the Greek letter lambda ($\lambda$) and is calculated using

$$\lambda = \frac{velocity}{f}$$

For electromagnetic radio waves, the velocity in air or vacuum is $c = 3 \times 10^8$ m/s, which is the speed of light.

The *phase angle* between two waveforms of the same frequency is the angular difference at a given instant of time.

Consider the sinusoidal waveforms in Figure 4-6. Wave *B* reaches its maximum value 90° ahead of wave *A*. Wave *B* is said to "lead" wave *A* by 90° or wave *A* is said to "lag" wave *B* by 90°.

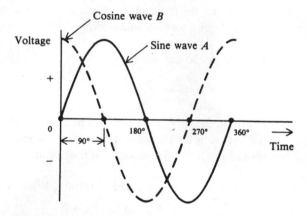

**Figure 4-6** Sinusoidal waveforms 90° out of phase.

# Phasors

To compare phase angles or phases of alternating voltages and currents, it is more convenient to use *phasor diagrams* corresponding to the waveforms.

A *phasor* is a quantity that has magnitude and direction (angle) that may vary with time.

The length of the phasor represents the maximum magnitude of the sinusoidal waveform while the angle with respect to the horizontal axis indicates the phase angle. One waveform can be chosen as a reference. Generally the reference phasor is horizontal, corresponding to 0°. Given the waveforms from Figure 4-6, either of the corresponding phasor diagrams of Figure 4-7 could be valid.

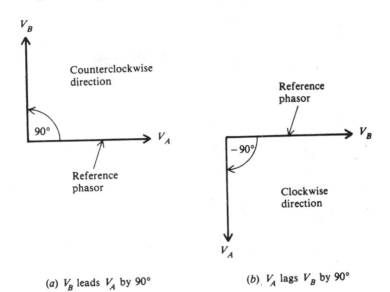

(a) $V_B$ leads $V_A$ by 90°          (b) $V_A$ lags $V_B$ by 90°

**Figure 4-7** Leading and lagging phase angles

When two waves are in phase (Figure 4-8(a)), the phase angle is zero. Then the amplitudes add (Figure 4-8(b)). When the two waves are exactly out of phase (Figure 4-9(a)), the phase angle is 180°. Their amplitudes subtract (Figure 4-9(b)). Equal value amplitude phasors that are 180° out of phase cancel each other.

**Example 4.3** What is the phase angle between waves $A$ and $B$ (Figure 4-10)? Draw the phasor diagram with wave $A$ as a reference.

(a) Waveforms         (b) Phasor diagram

**Figure 4-8** Two waves in phase with angle 0°

(a) Waveforms         (b) Phasor diagram

**Figure 4-9** Two waves in opposite phase with angle 180°

**Solution:** The phase angle is the angular distance between correspond-ing points on waves $A$ and $B$. Convenient corresponding points are max-ima, minima, and zero crossings for each wave. At the zero crossings on the horizontal axis (Figure 4-10), the phase angle $\theta = 30°$. Since wave $A$ reaches its zero crossing before wave $B$ does, $A$ leads $B$ or $B$ lags $A$. Though the phasors are not drawn to scale (Figure 4-11), $V_A$ is drawn smaller than $V_B$ because the maximum value of $V_A$ is less than that of $V_B$.

**Figure 4-10** Finding the phase angle between waves $A$ and $B$

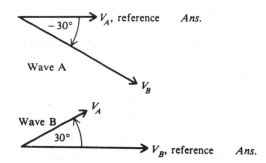

**Figure 4-11** Wave A as reference phasor ($V_B$ lags $V_A$ by 30°)

# Characteristic Values of Voltage, Current, and Power in AC Circuits

Since an ac sine wave voltage or current has many instantaneous values throughout the cycle, it is convenient to specify magnitudes for comparing one wave to another.

The *peak value* is the maximum value of $V_M$ or $I_M$.

The *peak-to-peak (p-p)* value is double the peak value when the positive and negative peaks are symmetrical.

The *average value* is the time average of a half cycle of the sine wave (average of a full cycle is zero). The average values are 0.637 times the peak values, i.e., $V_{av} = 0.637 V_M$ , $I_{av} = 0.637 I_M$

The *root-mean-square value* (**rms**) or *effective value* is 0.707 times the peak value, i.e., $V_{rms} = 0.707 V_M$ , $I_{rms} = 0.707 I_M$ .

The rms value of an alternating sine wave corresponds to the same amount of direct current in heating power. An alternating voltage with an rms value of 115 V, is just as effective in heating the filament of a light bulb as 115 V from a dc voltage source. Unless otherwise indicated, all sine wave ac measurements are given in rms values. The letters $V$ and $I$ are used to denote rms voltage and current. For instance, $V =$ 220 V (an ac power line voltage) is understood to mean 220 V rms. Table 4-1 shows conversions from one characteristic value to another.

**Table 4.1 Conversion Table for AC Sine Waves**

| Multiply the Value | By | To Get the Value |
|---|---|---|
| Peak | 2 | Peak-to-peak |
| Peak-to-peak | 0.5 | Peak |
| Peak | 0.637 | Average |
| Average | 1.570 | Peak |
| Peak | 0.707 | RMS (effective) |
| RMS (effective) | 1.414 | Peak |
| Average | 1.110 | RMS (effective) |
| RMS (effective) | 0.901 | Average |

**Example 4.4** A commercial ac power-line voltage is 240 V. What are the peak and p-p voltages?

**Solution:** Using Table 4.1,

$$V_M = 1.414\, V_{rms} = 1.414(240) = 339.4 \text{ V}$$

$$V_{p-p} = 2\, V_M = 2(339.4) = 678.8 \text{ V}$$

In an ac circuit with only resistance, the voltage and current are in phase and that allows the use of dc analysis techniques with the rms values.

**Example 4.5** A 110-V ac voltage is applied across the series resistances (Figure 4-12). Find the current, voltage drop, and power dissipated in each resistor.

**Figure 4-12** AC analysis of resistors in series

**Solution:** The total resistance is

$$R_T = R_1 + R_2 = 5 + 15 = 20 \text{ }\Omega$$

The current is the same through both since they are in series. The current is

$$I = \frac{V}{R_T} = \frac{110}{20} = 5.5 \text{ A}$$

Using Ohm's law, the voltage drops are

$$V_1 = IR_1 = 5.5(5) = 27.5 \text{ V}$$

$$V_2 = IR_2 = 5.5(15) = 82.5 \text{ V}$$

The dissipated powers are

$$P_1 = I^2 R_1 = (5.5)^2 (5) = 151.25 \text{ W}$$

$$P_2 = I^2 R_2 = (5.5)^2 (15) = 453.75 \text{ W}$$

Again, a reminder that the voltages and current in Example 4.5 were specified in rms values.

## IMPORTANT THINGS TO REMEMBER:

✓ An ac voltage is one that continually changes in magnitude and periodically reverses polarity.

✓ An ac voltage can be produced by a generator, called an alternator.

✓ When a sine wave of alternating voltage is connected across a load resistance, the current that flows in the circuit is also a sine wave.

✓ One cycle per second is one hertz. The amount of time for the completion of one cycle is the period.

✓ A *phasor* is a quantity that has magnitude and direction (angle) that may vary with time.

✓ When two waveforms are in-phase, the amplitudes of the phasors add directly. When they are in opposite-phase (phase difference is 180°), the amplitudes subtract.

✓ The peak value is the maximum value of $V_M$ or $I_M$.

✓ The peak-to-peak (p-p) value is double the peak value when the positive and negative peaks are symmetrical.

✓ The root-mean-square value (rms) or effective value is 0.707 times the peak value, i.e., $V_{rms} = 0.707 \, V_M$, $I_{rms} = 0.707 \, I_M$.

✓ In an ac circuit with only resistance, the voltage and current are in-phase and that allows the use of dc analysis techniques with the rms values.

## Solved Problems

**Solved Problem 4.1** For an ac signal, calculate the time delay $t$ for a phase angle of 45° at a frequency of 500 Hz.

**Solution:** Find the period that corresponds to the time for one cycle of 360°, and then find the proportional part of the period that corresponds to 45°.

$$T = \frac{1}{f} = \frac{1}{500} = 0.02 \text{ s} = 2 \text{ ms}$$

At $\theta = 45°$, $\qquad t = \frac{45°}{360°}(2) = 0.25 \text{ ms}$

**Solved Problem 4.2** A 120-V ac voltage is applied across a $20 - \Omega$ resistive load (Figure 4-13). Find values of $I$, $V_M$, $V_{p-p}$, $V_{av}$, $I_M$, $I_{p-p}$, $I_{av}$, and $P$.

$V = 120$ V      $R_L$   20 $\Omega$

**Figure 4-13** AC source with single resistive load

**Step 1:** Using Ohm's law,

$$I = \frac{V}{R_L} = \frac{120}{20} = 6 \text{ A}$$

**Step 2:** Using Table 4-1 to calculate voltage and current values:

$$V_M = 1.414V = 1.414(120) = 169.7 \text{ V}$$

$$V_{p-p} = 2V_M = 2(169.7) = 339.4 \text{ V}$$

$$V_{av} = 0.637V_M = (0.637)(169.7) = 108.3 \text{ V}$$

$$I_M = 1.414I = 1.414(6) = 8.5 \text{ A}$$

$$I_{p-p} = 2I_M = 2(8.5) = 17 \text{ A}$$

$$I_{av} = 0.637I_M = (0.637)(8.5) = 5.4 \text{ A}$$

$$P = I^2 R_L = 6^2(20) = 720 \text{ W}$$

*or*

$$P = \frac{V^2}{R_L} = \frac{120^2}{20} = 720 \text{ W}$$

*or*

$$P = VI = 120(6) = 720 \text{ W}$$

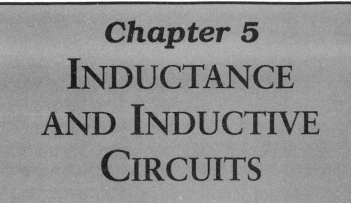

# Chapter 5
# INDUCTANCE AND INDUCTIVE CIRCUITS

IN THIS CHAPTER:

✔ *Inductance of Coils*
✔ *Inductive Reactance*
✔ *Inductive Circuits*
✔ *Transformers*
✔ *Solved Problems*

## Inductance of Coils

The ability of a conductor to induce a voltage in itself when the current changes is its *self-inductance*, or simply *inductance*. The symbol for inductance is $L$. The unit of inductance is the henry (H).

One henry is the amount of inductance that permits one volt to be induced when the current changes at the rate of one ampere per second (Figure 5-1). Conducting coils are commonly used to build circuit components called *inductors* at a specified inductance $L$. The self-induced voltage for an inductor is

$$v_L = L\frac{\Delta i}{\Delta t} \qquad (5\text{-}1)$$

where $\Delta i/\Delta t$ is the rate of change of the current (A/s).

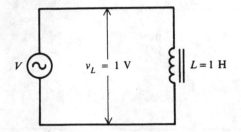

**Figure 5-1** The inductance of a coil is 1 H when a change
of 1 A/s induces 1 V across the coil

**Example 5.1** A coil has an inductance of $50\,\mu\text{H}$ . What voltage is
induced across the inductor when the rate of change of the current is $-10$
000 A/s?

**Solution:** Using (5-1),

$$v_L = L\frac{\Delta i}{\Delta t} = (50\times 10^{-6})(10^4) = 0.5\ \text{V}$$

When the current in a conductor or coil changes, the varying flux
can cut across any other conductor or coil nearby, thus inducing voltages in both. A varying current in $L_1$, therefore, induces a voltage across
$L_1$ and across $L_2$ (Figure 5-2). When the induced voltage $v_{L2}$

Magnetic flux

**Figure 5-2** Mutual inductance between $L_1$ and $L_2$

produces current in $L_2$, its varying magnetic field induces a voltage in $L_1$.

Hence, the two coils $L_1$ and $L_2$ have ***mutual inductance*** because current change in one coil can induce voltage in the other. The unit of mutual inductance is also the henry. The symbol for mutual inductance is $L_M$.

Two coils have $L_M$ of 1 H when a current change of 1 A/s in one coil induces 1 V in the other coil. The schematic symbols for two coils with mutual inductance are shown in Figure 5-3.

(*a*) Air core          (*b*) Iron core

**Figure 5-3** Schematic symbols for two coils with mutual inductance

A coil's inductance depends on how it is wound, the core material on which it is wound, the number of turns of wire with which it is wound, and the length of the coil.

* Inductance $L$ increases as the number of turns of wire $N$ around the core increases. Inductance increases as the square of the turns increases. For example, if the number of turns is doubled, inductance increases by 4 times, assuming the area and length of the coil remain constant.
* Inductance increases as the relative permeability $\mu_r$ of the core material increases.
* As the area $A$ enclosed by each turn increases, the inductance increases. Since the area is a function of the square of the diameter of the coil, inductance increases as the square of the diameter.

- Inductance decreases as the length of the coil increases (assuming the number of turns remains constant).

Losses in the magnetic core are due to *eddy-current* losses and *hysteresis losses*. Eddy-currents flow within the core material itself and dissipate at heat in the core. They can be reduced by using insulating materials in the core. Hysteresis losses arise from additional power needed to reverse the magnetic field in magnetic materials with alternating current. Hysteresis losses generally are less than eddy-current losses. Air-core coils suffer almost no loss at all.

## Inductive Reactance

*Inductive reactance* $X_L$ is the opposition to ac current due to the inductance in the circuit. The unit of inductive reactance is the ohm ($\Omega$) .

The formula for inductive reactance is

$$X_L = 2\pi f L \qquad (5\text{-}2)$$

where $f$ is the frequency and $L$ is the inductance. In a circuit containing only an inductor and a voltage source (Figure 5-4), Ohm's law can be used to find current and voltage by substituting $X_L$ for $R$.

**Figure 5-4** Circuit with only $X_L$

**Example 5.2** The primary coil of a power transformer has an inductance of 30 mH with negligible resistance (Figure 5-5). Find its inductive reactance at 60 Hz and the current it will draw from a 120 V line.

**Figure 5-5** $X_L$ circuit for Example 5.2

**Solution:** Find $X_L$ by using (5-2) and the $I_L$ by using Ohm's law

$$X_L = 2\pi f L = 6.28(60)(30 \times 10^{-3}) = 11.3 \ \Omega$$

$$I_L = \frac{V_L}{X_L} = \frac{120}{11.3} = 10.6 \ \text{A}$$

If inductors are spaced sufficiently far apart so that they do not interact electromagnetically with each other, their values can be combined just like resistors when connected together.

If inductors are connected in series (Figure 5-6), the total inductance is the sum of the individual inductances

$$L_T = L_1 + L_2 + L_3 + \cdots + L_n \qquad (5\text{-}3)$$

**Figure 5-6** Inductances in series without mutual coupling

If two series-connected coils are spaced closely together so that there is *significant mutual coupling*, the total inductance will be

$$L_T = L_1 + L_2 \pm 2L_M \qquad\qquad (5\text{-}4)$$

where $L_M$ is the mutual inductance between the two coils. The plus (+) sign in (5-4) is used if the coils are arranged in *series-adding* form (Figure 5-7(*a*)). The minus (–) sign is used if the coils are arranged in *series-opposing* form (Figure 5-7(*b*)). The difference between series-adding and series-opposing is the winding direction being reversed in $L_2$ (Figure 5-7). The large dots above the coils (Figure 5-7) are used to indicate the polarity of the winding without having to show the physical construction.

    If inductors are spaced sufficiently far apart so the mutual inductance is negligible, the rules for combining inductors in parallel are the same as for resistors.

    If a number of inductors are connected in *parallel* (Figure 5-8), their total inductance is

$$\frac{1}{L_T} = \frac{1}{L_1} + \frac{1}{L_2} + \frac{1}{L_3} + \cdots + \frac{1}{L_n} \qquad\qquad (5\text{-}5)$$

**Figure 5-7** $L_1$ and $L_2$ in series with mutual coupling $L_M$

**Figure 5-8** Inductances in parallel without mutual coupling

The total inductance of two inductors are connected in *parallel* is

$$L_T = \frac{L_1 L_2}{L_1 + L_2} \tag{5-6}$$

**Example 5.3** A 10 H and a 12 H inductor are connected in series (neglect mutual inductance). What is the total inductance?

**Solution:** Using (5-3),

$$L_T = L_1 + L_2 = 10 + 12 = 22 \text{ H}$$

**Example 5.4** The two inductors of Example 5.3 are moved close together so that they now have $L_M = 7\,\text{H}$. What is the total inductance if they are wound in the same direction?

**Solution:** If they are wound in the same direction that corresponds to "series-adding," the "+"-form of (5-4) is used to find $L_T$:

$$L_T = L_1 + L_2 + 2L_M = 10 + 12 + 2(7) = 36\ H$$

**Example 5.5** What is the total inductance of two parallel inductors with values of 8 H and 12 H?

**Solution:** Using (5-6),

$$L_T = \frac{L_1 L_2}{L_1 + L_2} = \frac{8(12)}{8 + 12} = \frac{96}{20} = 4.8 \text{ H}$$

## Inductive Circuits

If an ac voltage $v$ is applied across a circuit having *only* inductance (Figure 5-9), *the resulting current* $i_L$ *will lag the voltage across the inductance* $v_L$ *by* 90° (Figure 5-10).

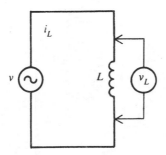

**Figure 5-9** AC voltage applied across an inductor

(*a*)                                (*b*)
**Figure 5-10** Inductor voltage and current: (*a*) time diagram; (*b*) phasor diagram

When a coil has a series resistance (Figure 5-11(*a*)), the rms current $I$ is limited by both $X_L$ and $R$ since they are in series. The voltage drop across $R$ is $V_R = IR$, and the voltage drop across $X_L$ is $V_L = IX_L$. The current through $X_L$ must lag $V_L$ by 90° because this is the phase angle between current through an inductance and its self-induced voltage (Figure 5-11($b$)). The current $I$ through $R$ and its $IR$ voltage drop are in-phase so the phase angle is 0° (Figure 5-11($b$)).

(*a*) Circuit    (*b*) Phasor diagram

**Figure 5-11** $R$ and $X_L$ in series.

To combine two waveforms out-of-phase, we add their equivalent phasors. The method is to add the tail of one phasor to the arrowhead of the other, using angle to show their relative phase. The sum of the phasors is a resultant phasor from the start of one phasor to the end of the other phasor.

## ⭐ Note!

Since the $V_R$ and $V_L$ phasors form a right triangle, *the resultant phasor will be the hypotenuse of the triangle* (Figure 5-12).

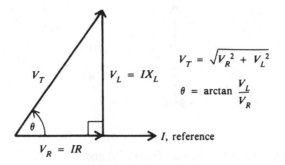

**Figure 5-12** Phasor voltage triangle

Therefore the resultant is

$$V_T = \sqrt{V_R^2 + V_L^2} \tag{5-7}$$

where the total voltage is the phasor sum of $V_R$ and $V_L$ which are 90° out-of-phase. All voltages must be in the same units. For example, when $V_R$ and $V_L$ are rms values, $V_T$ is also rms. Most of the ac calculations will be made in rms units.

The phase angle $\theta$ between $V_T$ and $V_R$ is (Figure 5-12)

$$\theta = \arctan \frac{V_L}{V_R} \tag{5-8}$$

Since $V_R$ is in phase with $I$, $\theta$ is also the phase angle between $V_T$ and $I$ where $I$ lags $V_T$.

The resultant of the phasor addition of $R$ and $X_L$ is called **imped-ance**. The symbol for impedance is $Z$. The impedance unit is ohms ($\Omega$).

Impedance is the total opposition to the flow of current. The impedance triangle (Figure 5-13) corresponds to the voltage triangle (Figure 5-12) but the common factor $I$ cancels.

**Figure 5-13** Phasor addition of $R$ and $X_L$ to find $Z$

The equations for impedance and phase angle are derived as follows:

$$V_T^2 = V_R^2 + V_L^2$$

$$(IZ)^2 = (IR)^2 + (IX_L)^2$$

$$Z^2 = R^2 + X_L^2$$

$$Z = \sqrt{R^2 + X_L^2} \tag{5-9}$$

$$\theta = \arctan \frac{X_L}{R} \tag{5-10}$$

**Example 5.6** For the series $RL$ circuit (Figure 5-14($a$)), find the following: $Z$, $\theta$ , $I$, $V_R$, and $V_L$.

**Solution:** Use the following steps:
**Step 1:** Find $Z$ and $\theta$ using (5-9) and (5-10) (see Figure 5-14($b$)):

$$Z = \sqrt{R^2 + X_L^2} = \sqrt{50^2 + 70^2} = \sqrt{2500 + 4900} = \sqrt{7400} = 86 \, \Omega$$

$$\theta = \arctan \frac{X_L}{R} = \arctan \frac{70}{50} = \arctan 1.4 = 54.5°$$

Therefore, $V_T$ leads $I$ by 54.5° (see Figure 5-14($c$)).

**Step 2:** Find $I$, $V_R$ , $V_L$

$$I = \frac{V_T}{Z} = \frac{120}{86} = 1.4 \text{ A}$$

$$V_R = IR = 1.4(50) = 70.0 \text{ V}$$

$$V_L = IX_L = 1.4(70) = 98.0 \text{ V}$$

$I$ and $V_R$ are in phase. $V_L$ leads $I$ by 90° (see Figure 5-14($d$)).

To check, show that the phasor sum of $V_R$ and $V_L$ equal $V_T$ (Figure 5-14($e$)) using (5-7):

$$V_T = \sqrt{V_R^2 + V_L^2} = \sqrt{70^2 + 98^2} \approx 120 \text{ V}$$

(the answer is not exactly 120 V due to rounding off $I$ ). Therefore, the calculations check out.

For parallel circuits with $R$ and $X_L$ (Figure 5-15), the same applied voltage $V_T$ is across both components since they are in parallel. There is no phase difference between the component voltages so $V_T$ will be used as the reference phasor. The resistive branch current $I_R = V_T/R$ is in phase with $V_T$. The inductive branch current $I_L = V_T/X_L$ lags $V_T$ by 90° (Figure 5-16) because the current in an inductance lags the voltage across it by 90°. The phasor sum of $I_R$ and $I_L$ equals the total line current $I_T$ (Figure 5-17) or

$$I_T = \sqrt{I_R^2 + I_L^2} \qquad (5\text{-}11)$$

$$\theta = \arctan\left(-\frac{I_L}{I_R}\right) \qquad (5\text{-}12)$$

(a) Series *RL* circuit

(b)

(c)

(d)

(e)

**Figure 5-14** Series *RL* circuit for Example 5.6

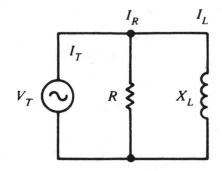

**Figure 5-15** Parallel *RL* circuit

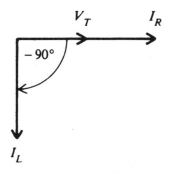

**Figure 5-16** Phasor diagram for parallel *RL* circuit

**Figure 5-17** Current-phasor triangle

For the general case of calculating the total impedance $Z_T$ of $R$ and $X_L$ in parallel, assume any number for the applied voltage $V_T$ because in the calculation of $Z_T$ in terms of the branch currents, the value of $V_T$ cancels. A convenient value to assume for $V_T$ is the value of either $R$ or $X_L$, whichever is the higher number. This is only one method among others for calculating $Z_T$.

**Example 5.7** What is the impedance $Z_T$ of a 200 $\Omega$ $R$ in parallel with a

400 $\Omega$ $X_L$? Assume 400 V for the applied voltage $V_T$.

**Solution:** Calculate the branch currents:

$$I_R = \frac{V_T}{R} = \frac{400}{200} = 2 \text{ A}$$

$$I_L = \frac{V_T}{X_L} = \frac{400}{400} = 1 \text{ A}$$

Using (5-11),

$$I_T = \sqrt{I_R^2 + I_L^2} = \sqrt{4+1} = \sqrt{5} = 2.24 \text{ A}$$

Using Ohm's law,

$$Z_T = \frac{V_T}{I_T} = \frac{400}{2.24} = 178.6 \, \Omega$$

In an ac circuit with inductive reactance, the line current $I$ lags the applied voltage $V$.

The **real power P** is equal to the voltage multiplied by only that portion of the line current which is in-phase with the voltage.
Therefore,

$$\text{Real power } P = V\,I\,\cos\theta \tag{5-13}$$

where $\theta$ is the phase angle between $V$ and $I$ and $\cos\theta$ is the *power factor* (PF) of the circuit. Also,

$$\text{Real power } P = I^2 R \tag{5-14}$$

where $R$ is the total resistive component of the circuit.

**Reactive power Q** in voltamperes reactive (VAR) is expressed as follows:

$$\text{Reactive power } Q = V\,I\,\sin\theta \tag{5-15}$$

**Apparent power S** is the product of $V$ and $I$. The unit is voltamperes (VA) and is given by:

$$\text{Apparent power } S = V\,I \tag{5-16}$$

In all power formulas, the $V$ and $I$ are rms values. The phasor diagram of power (Figure 5-18) can illustrate the relationships of real, reactive, and apparent power.

**Figure 5-18** Power triangle for *RL* circuits

**Example 5.8** The ac circuit (Figure 5-19) has 2 A through the given $R$ and $X_L$. Find the power factor, the applied voltage $V$, real power $P$, reactive power $Q$, and the apparent power $S$.

**Solution:** Use the following steps:

**Step 1:** Find the phase angle $\theta$, $\cos\theta$, and impedance $Z$ by the impedance triangle (Figure 5-20).

$$\theta = \arctan \frac{X_L}{R} = \arctan \frac{100}{173} = \arctan 0.578 = 30°$$

The power factor is

$$PF = \cos\theta = \cos 30° = 0.866$$

and the impedance is

$$Z = \sqrt{R^2 + X_L^2} = 200 \, \Omega$$

**Step 2:** Find $V$.

$$V = IZ = 2(200) = 400 \text{ V}$$

**Figure 5-19** Power in series $RL$ circuit

**Figure 5-20** Impedance triangle

**Step 3:** Find $P$ using (5-13) or (5-14).

$$P = I^2 R = 2^2(173) = VI \cos\theta = 400(2)(\cos 30°) = 692 \text{ W}$$

**Step 4:** Find $Q$ and $S$ using (5-15) and (5-16).

$$Q = VI \sin\theta = 400(2)(\sin 30°) = 400 \text{ VAR lagging}$$

The reactive power in an inductive circuit is "lagging" because $I$ lags $V$.

$$S = VI = 400(2) = 800 \text{ VA}$$

See Figure 5-21 for the power triangle.

**Figure 5-21** Power triangle for Example 5.8

# Transformers

The basic transformer consists of two coils electrically insulated from each other and wound upon a common core (Figure 5-22). Magnetic coupling is used to transfer electric energy from one coil to another.

## You Need to Know ✔

The coil which *receives* energy from an ac source is called the *primary*. The coil which *delivers* energy to an ac load is called the *secondary*.

The core of transformers used at low frequencies is generally made of magnetic material, usually sheet steel. Cores of transformers used at higher frequencies are made of powdered iron and ceramics or non-magnetic materials.

**Figure 5-22** Simple diagram of a transformer

The *voltage ratio* $V_p/V_s$ *(VR)* is directly proportional to the number of turns on the coils. The relationship is expressed by the formula

$$\frac{V_p}{V_s} = \frac{N_p}{N_s} \qquad (5\text{-}17)$$

where $N_p$ and $N_s$ are the number of turns in the primary and secondary coils, respectively. The ratio $N_p/N_s$ is the *turns ratio (TR)*.

A voltage ratio of 1:4 (read as "1 to 4") means that for each volt on the transformer primary, there is 4 V on the secondary. When the secondary voltage is greater than the primary voltage, the transformer is called a *step-up transformer*. When the secondary voltage is less than the primary, the transformer is called a *step-down transformer*.

**Example 5.9** An iron-core transformer operating from a 120-V line has 500 turns on the primary and 100 on the secondary. Find the secondary voltage.

**Solution:** Using (5-17),

$$V_s = \frac{N_s}{N_p}V_p = \frac{100}{500}120 = 24 \text{ V}$$

The current in the coils of a transformer is inversely proportional to the voltage in the coils. This relationship is

$$\frac{I_s}{I_p} = \frac{V_p}{V_s}$$

(5-18)

where $I_p$ and $I_s$ are the currents in the primary and secondary coils, respectively.

Substituting (5-17), we get

$$\frac{I_s}{I_p} = \frac{N_p}{N_s}$$

(5-19)

**Example 5.10** A bell transformer with 240 turns on the primary and 30 turns on the secondary draws 0.3 A from a 120-V line. Find the secondary current.

**Solution:** Using (5-19),

$$I_s = \frac{N_p}{N_s}I_p = \frac{240}{30}(0.3) = 2.4 \text{ A}$$

Maximum power is transferred from one circuit to another when the impedances of the two circuits are equal or *matched*.

A transformer can perform an *impedance-matching* function. The turns ratio establishes the proper relationship between the ratio of the primary and secondary winding impedances. This relationship is expressed as

$$\left(\frac{N_p}{N_s}\right)^2 = \frac{Z_p}{Z_s}$$

(5-20)

**Example 5.11** Find the turns ratio of a transformer used to match a $20-\Omega$ load to a $72\,000-\Omega$ load.

**Solution:** Using (5-20),

$$\frac{N_p}{N_s} = \sqrt{\frac{Z_p}{Z_s}} = \sqrt{\frac{20}{72000}} = \sqrt{\frac{1}{3600}} = \frac{1}{60} = 1:60$$

An *autotransformer* is a special type of transformer which only has one winding (Figure 5-23). By *tapping*, or connecting, at points along the length of the winding, different voltages may be obtained.

The simplicity of the autotransformer makes it economical and space-saving. However, it does not provide electrical isolation between primary and secondary circuits.

**Figure 5-23** Autotransformer schematic diagram

The symbol for a transformer gives no indication of the phase of the voltage across the secondary since the phase depends on the direction of the windings. To solve this problem, polarity dots are used to indicate the phase of the primary and secondary signals. The voltages are either *in-phase* (Figure 5-24(a)) or 180° *out-of-phase* with respect to the primary voltage (Figure 5-24(b)).

(a) Voltages in phase       (b) Voltages out of phase

**Figure 5-24** Polarity notation of transformer coils

# IMPORTANT THINGS TO REMEMBER:

✓ If enough energy is applied, some of the outermost valence electrons will leave an atom as free electrons. It is the movement of free electrons that provides electric current in conductors.

✓ The ability of a conductor to induce a voltage in itself when the current changes is its inductance.

✓ Two coils $L_1$ and $L_2$ have mutual inductance if a varying current in one coil can induce voltage in the other.

✓ Inductive reactance $X_L$ is the opposition to ac current due to the inductance in the circuit.

✓ Summary table for series and parallel RL circuits.

**Summary Table for Series and Parallel *RL* Circuits**

| $X_L$ and $R$ in Series | $X_L$ and $R$ in Parallel |
|---|---|
| $I$ the same in $X_L$ and $R$ <br> $V_T = \sqrt{V_R^2 + V_L^2}$ <br> $Z = \sqrt{R^2 + X_L^2} = \dfrac{V_T}{I}$ <br> $V_R$ lags $V_L$ by 90° <br> $\theta = \arctan \dfrac{X_L}{R}$ | $V_T$ the same across $X_L$ and $R$ <br> $I_T = \sqrt{I_R^2 + I_L^2}$ <br> $Z_T = \dfrac{V_T}{I_T}$ <br> $I_L$ lags $I_R$ by 90° <br> $\theta = \arctan \left( -\dfrac{I_L}{I_R} \right)$ |

# IMPORTANT THINGS TO REMEMBER:

✓ In a circuit with inductive reactance,
  Real power $P = V I \cos\theta$.

✓ In a circuit with inductive reactance,
  Reactive power $Q = V I \sin\theta$.

✓ In a circuit with inductive reactance,
  Apparent power $S = V I$.

✓ The voltage ratio $V_p/V_s$ of a transformer is proportional to the turns ratio $N_p/N_s$.

✓ The current ratio $I_s/I_p$ of a transformer is inversely proportional to the turns ratio $N_p/N_s$.

✓ The impedance ratio $Z_p/Z_s$ is proportional to the square of the turns ratio $(N_p/N_s)^2$.

## Solved Problems

**Solved Problem 5.1** A 120-Hz 20-mA current is present in a 10-H inductor. What is the reactance and the voltage drop across the inductor?

**Solution:**

$$X_L = 2\pi f L = (6.28)(120)(10) = 7536 \ \Omega$$

$$V_L = I \ X_L = (0.02)(7536) = 150.7 \ V$$

**Solved Problem 5.2** With two coils $L_1$ and $L_2$ as wound (Figure 5-25), find the total inductance.

**Figure 5-25** Coils for Solved Problem 5.2

**Solution:** Since the coils are wound in the same direction relative to the dots, $L_1$ and $L_2$ are series aiding. Then using the "+" sign in (5-4) gives

$$L_T = L_1 + L_2 + 2L_M = 9 + 13 + 2(3) = 28 \ H$$

**Solved Problem 5.3** A tuning coil has an inductance of 39.8 $\mu$H   and an internal resistance of 20 $\Omega$ . Find its impedance at a frequency of 100 kHz and the current through the coil if the voltage drop is 80 V across the entire coil.

**Step 1:** A coil with $R_i$ and $X_L$ is treated as a series $RL$ circuit. Begin by finding $X_L$ and then $Z$, $\theta$ .

$$X_L = 2\pi f L = (6.28)(100\times10^3)(39.8\times10^{-6}) = 25\ \Omega$$

$$Z = \sqrt{R_i^2 + X_L^2} = \sqrt{20^2 + 25^2} = 32\ \Omega$$

$$\theta = \arctan\frac{X_L}{R_i} = \arctan\frac{25}{20} = \arctan 1.25 = 51.3°$$

**Step 2:** Find $I$.

$$I = \frac{V}{Z} = \frac{80}{32} = 2.5\ \text{A}$$

# Chapter 6
# CAPACITANCE AND CAPACITIVE CIRCUITS

## Capacitance

A *capacitor* is an electrical device which typically consists of two conducting plates or cylinders of metal separated by an insulating material called a *dielectric* (Figure 6-1(*a*)). The schematic symbols for capacitors are shown in Figure 6-1(*b,c*).

(a) Structure      (b) Fixed      (c) Variable

**Figure 6-1** Capacitor and schematic symbols

A capacitor stores electric charge on the plates surrounding the dielectric. In the absence of an external source, the plates have the same amount of positive and negative charge and are said to be *charge neutral*. With the switch open (Figure 6-2(a)), the battery is not allowed to place excess charge on the plates and, hence, the plates of the capacitor remain charge neutral. When the switch is set to the closed position (Figure 6-2(b)), charge is allowed to flow through the wires and excess positive charge is deposited on plate A and an equal magnitude of negative charge is deposited on plate B. The movement of charge continues until the voltage across the plate equals the voltage of the battery. The capacitor is now *charged*. The insulating material between the plates prevents flow of charge directly from one plate to another. For this reason, the stored charge will remain even if the battery is removed and will remain charged until a conducting path allows flow of charge between the plates (Figure 6-3(a)). If a passive conducting material is placed across the plates without the source, charge will flow and the plates will revert to being charge neutral (Figure 6-3(b)). The capacitor is then said to be *discharged*.

(*a*) neutral capacitor          (*b*) charged capacitor

**Figure 6-2** Charging a capacitor

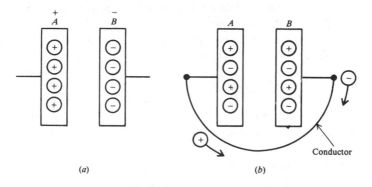

(*a*)                              (*b*)

**Figure 6-3** Discharging a capacitor

⭐ **Note!**

*Capacitance* is a measure of the ability to store an electric charge. The unit of capacitance is the farad (F). The farad is the capacitance that will store one coulomb of charge on the positive plate when the voltage applied across the capacitor terminals is one volt.

In equation form, capacitance

$$C = \frac{Q}{V} \tag{6-1}$$

where $Q$ is the amount of charge on the positive plate in coulombs and $V$ is the voltage across the plates in volts.

The characteristic of a dielectric that describes its ability to store energy is called the **dielectric constant**.

Air is used as a reference and is given a dielectric constant of 1. Some other dielectric materials are Teflon, paper, mica, Bakelite or ceramic. Paper, for example, has an average dielectric constant of 4, meaning it can provide for 4 times the stored charge in a capacitor versus that of an air-insulated capacitor of the same size.

The capacitance of a capacitor depends on the area of the conducting plates, the separation between the plates and the dielectric constant of the insulating material.

For a capacitor with two parallel plates, the formula to find its capacitance is

$$C = k \frac{A}{d}(8.85 \times 10^{-12}) \tag{6-2}$$

where $k$ is the dielectric constant of the insulating material, $A$ is the area of the plates in m$^2$, and $d$ is the separation of the plates in m.

Typical values for capacitance are in the $10^{-6}$ F to $10^{-12}$ F range. Therefore, it is often useful to use the units of microfarads $(1\,\mu F = 10^{-6}\ F)$, nanofarads $(1\,nF = 10^{-9}\ F)$, and picofarads $(1\,pF = 10^{-12}\ F)$.

**Example 6.1** The area of a two-plate mica capacitor is 0.0025 m$^2$ and the separation between plates is 0.02 m. If the dielectric constant of mica is 7, find the capacitance of the capacitor.

**Solution:** Using (6-2),

$$C = k \frac{A}{d}(8.85 \times 10^{-12}) = 7 \frac{0.0025}{0.02}(8.85 \times 10^{-12}) = 7.74 \times 10^{-12} = 7.74\ pF$$

Typically, commercial capacitors are named *according to their dielectric* (Table 6-1).

**Table 6-1 Types of Capacitors**

| Dielectric | Construction | Capacitance Range |
|---|---|---|
| Air | Meshed plates | 10–400 pF |
| Mica | Stacked sheets | 10–5000 pF |
| Paper | Rolled foil | 0.001–1 $\mu$F |
| Ceramic | Tubular | 0.5–1600 pF |
| | Disk | 0.002–0.1 $\mu$F |
| Electrolytic | Aluminum | 5–1000 $\mu$F |
| | Tantalum | 0.01–300 $\mu$F |

Most types of capacitors can be connected to an electric circuit without regard to polarity. But electrolytic capacitors and certain ceramic capacitors are marked to show which side must be connected to the more positive side of a circuit.

When $n$ capacitors are connected in *series* (Figure 6-4), the total capacitance $C_T$ is

$$\frac{1}{C_T} = \frac{1}{C_1} + \frac{1}{C_2} + \frac{1}{C_3} + \cdots + \frac{1}{C_n}$$

(6-3)

For 2 capacitors in series,

$$C_T = \frac{C_1 C_2}{C_1 + C_2}$$

(6-4)

**Figure 6-4** Capacitances in series

When capacitors are connected in *parallel* (Figure 6-5), the total capacitance $C_T$ is just the sum of the individual capacitances:

$$C_T = C_1 + C_2 + C_3 + \cdots + C_n \qquad (6\text{-}5)$$

**Figure 6-5** Capacitances in parallel

There is a limit to the voltage that may be applied across any capacitor. If an excessive voltage is applied, a current will be forced through the dielectric, sometimes burning a hole in it. The capacitor will then short-circuit and must be discarded.

## Remember

The maximum voltage that may be applied to a capacitor is called the ***working voltage*** and should not be exceeded.

**Example 6.2** Find the total capacitance of the series connected capacitors (Figure 6-6).

**Solution:** Using (6-3),

$$\frac{1}{C_T} = \frac{1}{C_1} + \frac{1}{C_2} + \frac{1}{C_3} = \frac{1}{3} + \frac{1}{5} + \frac{1}{10} = \frac{19}{30}$$

$$C_T = \frac{30}{19} = 1.6 \ \mu F$$

**Figure 6-6** Series capacitances for Example 6.2

## Capacitive Reactance

*Capacitive reactance* $X_C$ is the opposition to the flow of ac current due to the capacitance in the circuit. The unit of capacitive reactance is the ohm ($\Omega$) .

Capacitive reactance can be found by using the equation

$$X_C = \frac{1}{2\pi f C} \tag{6-6}$$

where $f$ is the frequency and $C$ is the capacitance.

Voltage and current in a circuit containing only capacitive reactance can be found using Ohm's law. However, in the case of a capacitive circuit, $R$ is replaced by $X_C$ .

$$V_C = I_C X_C$$

where $V_C$ is the voltage across the capacitor and $I_C$ is the current through the capacitor.

**Example 6.3** A 120 Hz 25-mA current flows in a circuit containing a 10 $\mu F$ capacitor (Figure 6-7). What is the voltage drop across the capacitor?

**Solution:** Find $X_C$ and $V_C$ using Ohm's law

**Figure 6-7** $X_C$ circuit for Example 6.3

$$X_C = \frac{1}{2\pi f C} = \frac{1}{2\pi(120)(10 \times 10^{-6})} = 132.5\ \Omega$$

$$V_C = I_C X_C = (25 \times 10^{-3})(132.5) = 3.31\ V$$

## Capacitive Circuits

If an ac voltage $v$ is applied across a circuit having only capacitance (Figure 6-8), *the resulting ac current through the capacitance, $i_C$, will lead the voltage across the capacitance, $v_C$, by 90°* (Figure 6-9). (Quantities expressed as lowercase letters indicate instantaneous values.)

**Figure 6-8** AC voltage applied across a capacitor

Voltages $v$ and $v_C$ are the same because they are parallel . Both $i_C$ and $v_C$ are sine waves with the same frequency. In series circuits, the current $I_C$ is the horizontal phasor for reference (Figure 6-10) so the voltage $V_C$ can be considered to lag $I_C$ by 90°.

(*a*)                                   (*b*)

**Figure 6-9** Capacitor voltage and current: (*a*) time diagram; (*b*) phasor diagram

**Figure 6-10** Phasor diagram, $I_C$ reference

## 118 BASIC ELECTRICITY

**Note!**

As with inductive circuits, the combination of resistance and capacitive reactance (Figure 6-11(a)) is called *impedance*.

(*a*) Circuit  (*b*) Phasor diagram

**Figure 6-11** $R$ and $X_C$ in series

In a series circuit containing $R$ and $X_C$, the same current $I$ flows through both. The voltage drop across $R$ is $V_R = IR$ , and the voltage drop across $X_C$ is $V_C = IX_C$ . The voltage across $X_C$ lags the current through $X_C$ by 90° (Figure 6-11(*b*)). The voltage across $R$ is in phase with $I$ since resistance does not produce any phase shift (Figure 6-11(*b*)).

To find the voltage $V_T$, we add phasors $V_R$ and $V_C$. Since they form a right triangle (Figure 6-12),

$$V_T = \sqrt{V_R^2 + V_C^2} \tag{6-7}$$

Note that the $IX_C$ phasor is downward, exactly opposite from an $IX_L$ phasor (see Figure 6-11) because of the opposite phase angle.

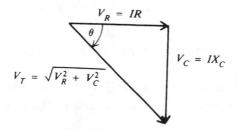

**Figure 6-12** Voltage-triangle phasor

The phase angle $\theta$ between $V_T$ and $V_R$ (Figure 6-12) is expressed according to the following equation:

$$\theta = \arctan\left(-\frac{V_C}{V_R}\right) \qquad (6\text{-}8)$$

The voltage triangle (Figure 6-12) corresponds to the impedance triangle (Figure 6-13) because the common factor $I$ in $V_R$ and $V_C$ cancels.

$$V_T^2 = V_R^2 + V_C^2$$

$$(IZ)^2 = (IR)^2 + (IX_C)^2$$

$$Z^2 = R^2 + X_C^2$$

$$Z = \sqrt{R^2 + X_C^2} \qquad (6\text{-}9)$$

$$\theta = \arctan\left(-\frac{X_C}{R}\right) \qquad (6\text{-}10)$$

**Figure 6-13** Series $RC$ impedance triangle

**Example 6.4** A 40 $\Omega$ $X_C$ and a 30 $\Omega$ $R$ are in series across a 120-V source (Figure 6-14(a)). Calculate $Z$, $I$, and $\theta$. Draw the phasor diagram.

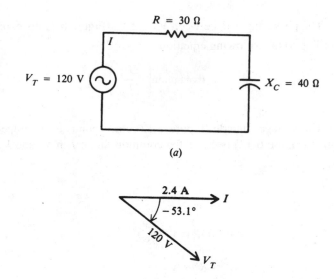

(a)

(b) Phasor diagram

**Figure 6-14** Series $RC$ circuit for Example 6.4

**Solution:** Using (6-9), the impedance is

$$Z = \sqrt{R^2 + X_C^2} = \sqrt{30^2 + 40^2} = \sqrt{2500} = 50\ \Omega$$

Using Ohm's law and (6-10),

$$I = \frac{V_T}{Z} = \frac{120}{50} = 2.4\ \text{A}$$

$$\theta = \arctan\left(-\frac{X_C}{R}\right) = \arctan\left(-\frac{40}{30}\right) = \arctan(-1.33) = -53.1°$$

See Figure 6-14(*b*) for the phasor diagram.

## Important

For parallel *RC* circuits (Figure 6-15), the voltage is the same across the source, *R* and $X_C$ .

The phasor diagram has the source voltage $V_T$ as the reference because it is the same throughout the circuit (Figure 6-16). The resistive branch current $I_R = V_T/R$ is in-phase with $V_T$. The capacitive branch current $I_C = V_T/X_C$ leads $V_T$ by 90°. The total line current $I_T$ equals the

phasor sum of $I_R$ and $I_C$ (Figure 6-17).

Figure 6-15 Parallel $RC$ circuit

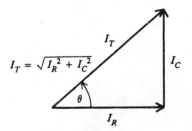

Figure 6-16 Phasor diagram for parallel $RC$ circuit

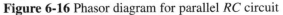

Figure 6-17 Current-triangle phasor

The total current is (using Figure 6-17)

$$I_T = \sqrt{I_R^2 + I_C^2}$$ (6-11)

$$\theta = \arctan \frac{I_C}{I_R}$$ (6-12)

The impedance of the parallel $RC$ circuit is

$$Z_T = \frac{V_T}{I_T}$$ (6-13)

**Example 6.5** A 15 $\Omega$ resistor and a capacitor of 20 $\Omega$ capacitive reactance are placed in parallel across a 120 V ac line (Figure 6-18(a)). Calculate $I_R$, $I_C$, $I_T$, $\theta$, and $Z_T$. Draw the phasor diagram.

(a)                                  (b) Phasor diagram

**Figure 6-18** Parallel *RC* circuit for Example 6.5

**Solution:** Using Ohm's law,

$$I_R = \frac{V_T}{R} = \frac{120}{15} = 8 \text{ A}$$

$$I_C = \frac{V_T}{X_C} = \frac{120}{20} = 6 \text{ A}$$

Using (6-11) and (6-12),

$$I_T = \sqrt{I_R^2 + I_C^2} = \sqrt{8^2 + 6^2} = \sqrt{100} = 10 \text{ A}$$

$$\theta = \arctan \frac{I_C}{I_R} = \arctan \frac{6}{8} = \arctan 0.75 = 36.9°$$

The total impedance is (6-13)

$$Z_T = \frac{V_T}{I_T} = \frac{120}{10} = 12 \text{ } \Omega$$

The phasor diagram is shown in Figure 6-18(*b*).

The power formulas given previously for *RL* circuits are equally applicable to *RC* circuits.

$$\text{Real power } P = V I \cos\theta \tag{6-14}$$

or

Real power $P = I^2 R$               (6-15)

Reactive power $Q = V I \sin\theta$        (6-16)

Apparent power $S = V I$            (6-17)

## IMPORTANT THINGS TO REMEMBER:

✓ A capacitor stores electric charge on the plates surrounding the dielectric.

✓ Capacitance is the ability to store an electric charge.

✓ The capacitance of a capacitor depends on the area of the conducting plates, the separation between the plates, and the dielectric constant of the insulating material.

✓ *Capacitive reactance* $X_C$ is the opposition to the flow of ac current due to the capacitance in the circuit.

✓ Summary table for series and parallel *RC* circuits

**Summary Table for Series and Parallel *RC* Circuits**

| $X_C$ and $R$ in Series | $X_C$ and $R$ in Parallel |
|---|---|
| $I$ the same in $X_C$ and $R$ | $V_T$ the same across $X_C$ and $R$ |
| $V_T = \sqrt{V_R^2 + V_C^2}$ | $I_T = \sqrt{I_R^2 + I_C^2}$ |
| $Z = \sqrt{R^2 + X_C^2} = \dfrac{V_T}{I}$ | $Z_T = \dfrac{V_T}{I_T}$ |
| $V_C$ lags $V_R$ by 90° | $I_C$ leads $I_R$ by 90° |
| $\theta = \arctan\left(-\dfrac{X_C}{R}\right)$ | $\theta = \arctan\dfrac{I_C}{I_R}$ |

Capacitance, like inductance, consumes no power. The only part of the circuit consuming power is the resistance.

## Solved Problems

**Solved Problem 6.1** Find the total capacitance of the series circuit and

the capacitive reactance of the group of capacitors when used in a $60-$ Hz circuit (Figure 6-19)

**Figure 6-19** Series capacitance circuit for Solved Problem 6.1

**Solution:**

$$\frac{1}{C_T} = \frac{1}{C_1} + \frac{1}{C_2} + \frac{1}{C_3}$$

$$= \frac{1}{0.1} + \frac{1}{0.5} + \frac{1}{0.25}$$

$$C_T = \frac{0.5}{8} = 0.0625 \ \mu F$$

$$X_c = \frac{1}{2\pi f C_T} = \frac{0.159}{f C_T} = \frac{0.159}{60(0.0625 \times 10^{-6})} = 42\,400 \ \Omega$$

**Solved Problem 6.2** A capacitance of $3.53\,\mu F$ and a resistance of

40 Ω are connected in series across a 110-V 1.5-kHz ac source (Figure 6-20(a)). Find $X_C, Z, \theta, I, V_R, V_C$ and $P$. Draw the phasor diagram.

**Step 1:** Find $X_C$.

(a)

(b) Phasor diagram

$$X_C = \frac{1}{2\pi f C} = \frac{0.159}{(1.5 \times 10^3)(3.53 \times 10^{-6})} = 30 \, \Omega$$

**Figure 6-20** Series $RC$ circuit for Solved Problem 6.2

**Step 2:** Find $Z$ and $\theta$.

$$Z = \sqrt{R^2 + X_C^2} = \sqrt{40^2 + 30^2} = 50\ \Omega$$

$$\theta = \arctan\left(-\frac{X_C}{R}\right) = \arctan\left(-\frac{30}{40}\right) = \arctan(-0.75) = -36.9°$$

**Step 3:** Find $I$.

$$I = \frac{V_T}{Z} = \frac{110}{50} = 2.2\ \text{A}$$

**Step 4:** Find $V_R$ and $V_C$. Using Ohm's law,

$$V_R = IR = 2.2(40) = 88\ \text{V}$$

$$V_C = IX_C = 2.2(30) = 66\ \text{V}$$

**Step 5:** Find $P$.

$$P = I^2 R = (2.2)^2\,(40) = 193.6\ \text{W}$$

See Figure 6-20(*b)* for the phasor diagram.

# Chapter 7
# GENERAL RLC CIRCUITS

IN THIS CHAPTER:

✔ *Series RLC Circuit Analysis*
✔ *Parallel RLC Circuit Analysis*
✔ *Power and Power Factor*
✔ *Solved Problems*

## Series RLC Circuit Analysis

Current in a series circuit containing resistance, inductive reactance, and capacitive reactance (Figure 7-1) is determined by the total impedance of the combination and the applied voltage.

The current $I$ is the same in $R$, $X_L$, and $X_C$ since they are in series.

The voltage drop across each element is found by Ohm's law:

$$V_R = IR \qquad V_L = IX_L \qquad V_C = IX_C$$

The voltage across the resistance is in-phase with the current through the resistance (Figure 7-2). The voltage across the inductance leads the

128

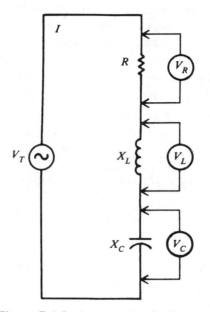

**Figure 7-1** Series *RLC* circuit diagram

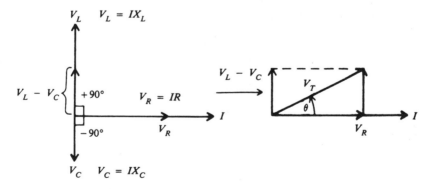

(*a*) Phasor diagram, $V_L > V_C$   (*b*) Voltage-phasor triangle, $V_L > V_C$

**Figure 7-2** *R*, $X_L$, and $X_C$ in series; $X_L > X_C$ for inductive circuit current through the inductance by 90° (Figure 7-2(a)). The voltage across the capacitance lags the current through the capacitance by 90° (Figure 7-2(a)). Since $V_L$ and $V_C$ are exactly 180° out-of-phase and acting in exactly opposite directions, they are added algebraically.

When $X_L$ is greater than $X_C$, the circuit is *inductive*, $V_L$ is greater than $V_C$ and $I$ lags $V_T$ (Figure 7-2(b)). The voltage-phasor triangle (Figure 7-2(b)) shows that the total applied voltage $V_T$ and phase angle are as follows:

$$V_T = \sqrt{V_R^2 + (V_L - V_C)^2} \qquad (7\text{-}1)$$

$$\theta = \arctan \frac{V_L - V_C}{V_R} \qquad (7\text{-}2)$$

When $X_C$ is greater than $X_L$, the circuit is *capacitive*, $V_C$ is greater than $V_L$ and $I$ leads $V_T$ (Figure 7-3). The voltage-phasor triangle (Figure 7-3(b)) shows that the total applied voltage $V_T$ and phase angle are as follows:

$$V_T = \sqrt{V_R^2 + (V_C - V_L)^2} \qquad (7\text{-}3)$$

$$\theta = \arctan \left( -\frac{V_C - V_L}{V_R} \right) \qquad (7\text{-}4)$$

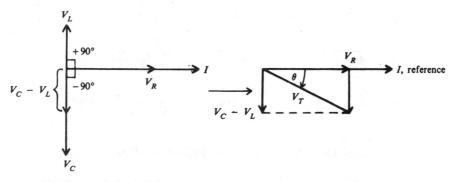

(a) Phasor diagram, $V_C > V_L$   (b) Voltage-phasor triangle, $V_C > V_L$

**Figure 7-3** $R$, $X_L$, and $X_C$ in series; $X_C > X_L$ for capacitive circuit

**Example 7.1** In an *RLC* series ac circuit (Figure 7-4(*a*)), find the applied voltage and phase angle. Draw the voltage-phasor diagram.

(a) Series *RLC* circuit

(b)  Voltage-phasor diagram

**Figure 7-4** Series *RLC* circuit from Example 7.1

**Solution:** By Ohm's law,

$$V_R = IR = 2(4) = 8\,\text{V}, V_L = IX_L = 2(19.5) = 39\,\text{V}, V_C = IX_C = 2(12) = 24\text{V}$$

Since $V_L > V_C$, (7-1) and (7-2) give

$$V_T = \sqrt{V_R^2 + (V_L - V_C)^2} = \sqrt{8^2 + (39 - 24)^2} = \sqrt{8^2 + 15^2} = 17 \text{ V}$$

$$\theta = \arctan \frac{V_L - V_C}{V_R} = \arctan \frac{39 - 24}{8} = \arctan \frac{15}{8} = \arctan 1.88 = 61.9°$$

The voltage-phasor diagram is shown in Figure 7-4(b).

The impedance Z is equal to the *phasor sum of R, $X_L$, and $X_C$.*

When $X_L > X_C$,

$$Z = \sqrt{R^2 + (X_L - X_C)^2} = \sqrt{R^2 + X^2} \qquad (7\text{-}5)$$

$$\theta = \arctan \frac{X}{R} \qquad (7\text{-}6)$$

where $X = X_L - X_C$ (Figure 7-5(a)).

When $X_C > X_L$,

$$Z = \sqrt{R^2 + (X_C - X_L)^2} = \sqrt{R^2 + X^2} \qquad (7\text{-}7)$$

$$\theta = \arctan -\frac{X}{R} \qquad (7\text{-}8)$$

where $-X = X_L - X_C$ (Figure 7-5(b)).

*(a)* $X_L > X_C$                                    *(b)* $X_C > X_L$

**Figure 7-5** Series *RLC* impedance-phasor triangles

**Example 7.2** Find the impedance of the series *RLC* circuit in Example 7.1

**Solution:** Since $X_L > X_C$, (7-5) and (7-6) give

$$X = X_L - X_C = 19.5 - 12 = 7.5\ \Omega$$

$$Z = \sqrt{R^2 + X^2} = \sqrt{4^2 + (7.5)^2} = 8.5\ \Omega$$

$$\theta = \arctan\frac{X}{R} = \arctan\frac{7.5}{4} = \arctan 1.875 = 61.9°$$

# Parallel RLC Circuit Analysis

A three-branch parallel ac circuit (Figure 7-6) has resistance in one branch, inductance in the second branch, and capacitance in the third branch.

The voltage is the same across all branches, $V_T = V_R = V_L = V_C$.

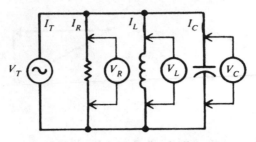

**Figure 7-6** Parallel *RLC* circuit diagram

$V_T$ is used as the reference to measure the phase angle $\theta$ . The total current $I_T$ is the phasor sum of the currents $I_R$, $I_L$, and $I_C$. The current in the resistance $I_R$ is in-phase with $V_T$ (Figure 7-7($a$)). The current in the inductance $I_L$ lags the voltage by 90°. The current in the capacitor $I_C$ leads the voltage $V_T$ by 90°. $I_L$ and $I_C$ are exactly 180° out-of-phase (Figure 7-7($a$)).

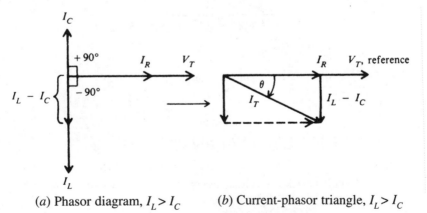

($a$) Phasor diagram, $I_L > I_C$          ($b$) Current-phasor triangle, $I_L > I_C$

**Figure 7-7** $R$, $X_L$, and $X_C$ in parallel; $I_L > I_C$ for inductive circuit

When $I_L > I_C$, $I_T$ lags $V_T$ so the parallel *RLC* is considered inductive (Fig 7-7($b$)). The current-phasor triangle (Figure 7-7($b$)) shows that the total current $I_T$ and phase angle are as follows:

$$I_T = \sqrt{I_R^2 + (I_L - I_C)^2}$$

(7-9)

$$\theta = \arctan\left(-\frac{I_L - I_C}{I_R}\right)$$

(7-10)

When $I_C > I_L$, $I_T$ leads $V_T$ so the parallel *RLC* is considered capacitive (Figure 7-8). The current-phasor triangle (Figure 7-8(*b*)) shows that the total current $I_T$ and phase angle are as follows:

$$I_T = \sqrt{I_R^2 + (I_C - I_L)^2}$$

(7-11)

$$\theta = \arctan\frac{I_C - I_L}{I_R}$$

(7-12)

(*a*) Phasor diagram, $I_C > I_L$      (*b*) Current-phasor triangle, $I_C > I_L$

**Figure 7-8** $R$, $X_L$, and $X_C$ in parallel; $I_C > I_L$ for capacitive circuit

In a parallel *RLC* circuit, when $X_L > X_C$, the capacitive current will be greater than the inductive current and the circuit is capacitive. When $X_C > X_L$, the inductive current will be greater than the capacitive current and the circuit is inductive.

# 136 BASIC ELECTRICITY

## ⭐ Note!

These relationships are opposite to those for a series *RLC* circuit.

The total impedance $Z_T$ of a parallel *RLC* circuit is given by

$$Z_T = \frac{V_T}{I_T}$$

$$(7\text{-}13)$$

**Example 7.3** A $400-\Omega$ resistor, a $50-\Omega$ inductive reactance and a $40-\Omega$ capacitive reactance are placed in parallel across a 120-V ac line (Figure 7-9(*a*)). Find the phasor branch currents, total current, phase angle, and impedance. Draw the phasor diagram.

(*a*)  Parallel *RLC* circuit

(*b*)  Phasor diagram

**Figure 7-9** Parallel *RLC* circuit from Example 7.3

**Solution:** Use the following steps:

**Step 1:** Find $I_R$, $I_L$, $I_C$ using Ohm's law.

$$I_R = \frac{V_T}{R} = \frac{120}{400} = 0.3\,\text{A} \qquad I_L = \frac{V_T}{X_l} = \frac{120}{50} = 2.4\,\text{A} \qquad I_C = \frac{V_T}{X_c} = \frac{120}{40} = 3\,\text{A}$$

**Step 2:** Since $I_C > I_L$, find $I_T, \theta$ using (7-11), (7-12).

$$I_T = \sqrt{I_R^2 + (I_C - I_L)^2} = \sqrt{(0.3)^2 + (3.0 - 2.4)^2}$$

$$I_T = \sqrt{(0.3)^2 + (0.6)^2} = 0.671\,\text{A}$$

$$\theta = \arctan \frac{3 - 2.4}{0.3} = \arctan \frac{0.6}{0.3} = \arctan 2 = 63.4°$$

**Step 3:** Find $Z_T$ using (7-13).

$$Z_T = \frac{V_T}{I_T} = \frac{120}{0.671} = 179\,\Omega$$

**Step 4:** Draw the phasor diagram (Figure 7-9($b$)). $I_T$ leads $V_T$.

Total current $I_T$ for a circuit containing parallel branches of $RL$ and $RC$ (Figure 7-10) is the phasor sum of branch currents $I_1$ and $I_2$. A convenient way to find $I_T$ is:

1. add algebraically the horizontal components of $I_1$ and $I_2$ with respect to the phasor reference $V_T$,
2. add algebraically the vertical components of $I_1$ and $I_2$, and
3. form a right triangle with these two sums as legs and calculate the value of the hypotenuse ($I_T$) and its angle to the horizontal.

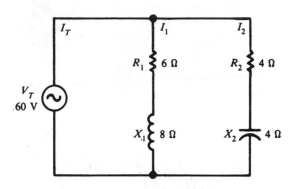

**Figure 7-10** Parallel *RL* and *RC* branches

**Example 7.4** An ac circuit has an *RL* branch parallel to an *RC* branch (Figure 7-10). Find the total current, phase angle, and impedance of this circuit.

**Solution:** Use the following steps:

**Step 1:** For the *RL* branch, find $Z_1, \theta_1$, and $I_1$.

$$Z_1 = \sqrt{R_1^2 + X_1^2} = \sqrt{6^2 + 8^2} = 10 \ \Omega$$

$$\theta_1 = \arctan \frac{X_1}{R_1} = \arctan \frac{8}{6} = 53.1°$$

$$I_1 = \frac{V_T}{Z_1} = \frac{60}{10} = 6 \ \text{A}$$

$I_1$ lags $V_T$ in the *RL* branch (inductive circuit) by 53.1°. Resolve $I_1$ into horizontal and vertical components with respect to $V_T$ (Figure 7-11):

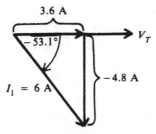

**Figure 7-11** Resolving inductive current $I_1$ into horizontal and vertical components

Horizontal component: $I_1 \cos\theta_1 = 6\cos(-53.1°) = 3.6$ A

Vertical component: $I_1 \sin\theta_1 = 6\sin(-53.1°) = -4.8$ A

**Step 2:** For the $RC$ branch, find $Z_2, \theta_2,$ and $I_2$.

$$Z_2 = \sqrt{R_2^2 + X_2^2} = \sqrt{4^2 + 4^2} = 5.66 \ \Omega$$

$$\theta_2 = \arctan\left(-\frac{X_2}{R_2}\right) = \arctan\left(-\frac{4}{4}\right) = -45°$$

$$I_2 = \frac{V_T}{Z_2} = \frac{60}{5.66} = 10.6 \text{ A}$$

$I_2$ leads $V_T$ in the $RC$ branch (capacitive circuit) by 45°. Resolve $I_2$ into horizontal and vertical components with respect to $V_T$ (Figure 7-12):

**Figure 7-12** Resolving capacitive current $I_2$ into horizontal
and vertical components

Horizontal component: $I_2 \cos\theta_2 = 10.6\cos(45°) = 7.5$ A

Vertical component: $I_2 \sin\theta_2 = 10.6\sin(45°) = 7.5$ A

**Step 3:** Find $I_T$. $I_T$ is the phasor sum of $I_1$ and $I_2$. Add the horizontal components of $I_1$ and $I_2$.

$$3.6 + 7.5 = 11.1 \text{ A}$$

Add the vertical components of $I_1$ and $I_2$.

$$-4.8 + 7.5 = 2.7 \text{ A}$$

The resultant phasor $I_T$ is (Figure 7-13)

$$I_T = \sqrt{(11.1)^2 + (2.7)^2} = \sqrt{130.5} = 11.4 \text{ A}$$

$$\theta = \arctan\frac{2.7}{11.1} = \arctan 0.243 = 13.7°$$

$$Z_T = \frac{V_T}{I_T} = \frac{60}{11.4} = 5.26 \ \Omega$$

Note that $I_T$ leads $V_T$ (Figure 7-13) so that the circuit is leading and thus capacitive.

**Figure 7-13** Resultant $I_T$ phasor for Example 7.4

# Power and Power Factor

The instantaneous power $p = vi$ at any instant in time.

When $v$ and $i$ are both positive or both negative, *their product is positive and power is expended throughout the cycle* (Figure 7-14).

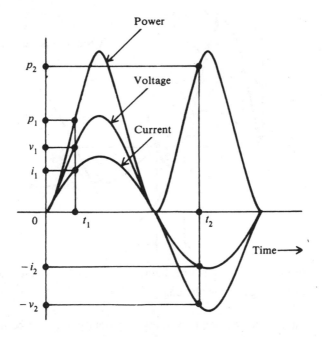

**Figure 7-14** Power-time diagram when $v$ and $i$ are in-phase

If $v$ is negative while $i$ is positive during any part of the cycle (Figure 7-15), or if $i$ is negative while $v$ is positive, their product will be negative. *This "negative" power is not available for work and is returned to the line.*

The product of voltage across the resistance and the current through the resistance is always positive and is called ***real power***. Real power can be considered as resistive power that is always dissipated as heat. Since the voltage across a reactance is always 90° out-of-phase with the current through the reactance, the product $p_x = v_x i_x$ is always negative. This product is called ***reactive power***. Similarly, the product of the line voltage and line current is known as ***apparent power***.

**Figure 7-15** Power-time diagram in series *RL* circuit where current lags voltage by angle $\theta$

Real power, reactive power, and apparent power can be represented by a right triangle (Figure 7-16).

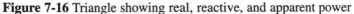

**Figure 7-16** Triangle showing real, reactive, and apparent power

From this triangle, the power formulas are:

Real power $P = V_R I_R = VI \cos\theta = I^2 R = \dfrac{V^2}{R}$,  W

$$(7\text{-}14)$$

Reactive power $Q = V_X I_X = VI \sin\theta$,  VAR

$$(7\text{-}15)$$

Apparent power $S = VI$,  VA

$$(7\text{-}16)$$

With line voltage $V$ as a reference phasor, in an inductive circuit, $S$ lags $P$ (Figure 7-17($a$)); while in a capacitive circuit, $S$ leads $P$ (Figure 7-17($b$)).

($a$) Lagging $PF$ (e.g., induction motor)

**Figure 7-17($a$)** Power triangles illustrating power factors

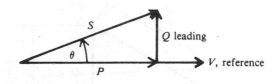

(b) Leading *PF* (e.g., bank of capacitors)

**Figure 7-17(b)** Power triangles illustrating power factors

# You Need to Know ✔

The ratio of real power to apparent power is called **the power factor (PF)** and is given by

$$PF = \frac{\text{real power } P}{\text{apparent power } S} = \frac{V_R I_R}{VI} = \frac{VI \cos\theta}{VI} = \cos\theta \qquad (7\text{-}17)$$

The power factor determines what portion of the apparent power is real power and can vary from 1 when the phase angle is 0° to 0 when $\theta = 90°$. A circuit in which the current lags the voltage (i.e., an inductive circuit) is said to have a **lagging PF**. A circuit in which the current leads the voltage (i.e., a capacitive circuit) is said to have a **leading PF**.

Power factor is expressed as a decimal or percentage. For example, a *PF* = 0.7 is the same as *PF* = 70%. At unity (*PF* = 1 = 100 %), the current and voltage are in phase and all available apparent power is being delivered to the load. A 70% *PF* means that the device only uses 70% of the apparent voltampere input. It is desirable to have the *PF* close to unity.

**Example 7.5** In the series *RLC* ac circuit from Example 7.1 (Figure 7-4($a$)), the line current of 2 A lags the applied voltage of 17 V by 61.9°. Find *PF*, *P*, *Q*, and *S*. Draw the power triangle.

**Solution:** $PF = \cos\theta = \cos 61.9° = 0.471$ or 47.1% lagging

$$P = VI \cos\theta = 17(2)(0.471) = 16 \text{ W}$$

$$Q = VI \sin\theta = 17(2)\sin 61.9° = 34(0.882) = 30 \text{ VAR}$$

$$S = VI = 17(2) = 34 \text{ VA}$$

The voltage triangle is shown in Figure 7-18.

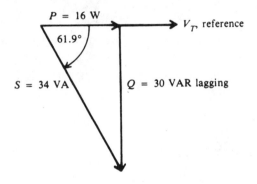

**Figure 7-18** Power triangle from Example 7.5

# IMPORTANT THINGS TO REMEMBER:

✓ If enough energy is applied, some of the outermost valence electrons will leave an atom as free electrons. It is the movement of free electrons that provides electric current in conductors.

✓ In a series $RLC$ circuit, when $X_L$ is greater than $X_C$, the circuit is *inductive*, $V_L$ is greater than $V_C$, and $I$ lags $V_T$.

✓ In a series $RLC$ circuit, when $X_C$ is greater than $X_L$, the circuit is *capacitive*, $V_C$ is greater than $V_L$, and $I$ leads $V_T$.

✓ In a parallel $RLC$ circuit, when $X_L > X_C$, the capacitive current will be greater than the inductive current and the circuit is capacitive.

✓ In a parallel $RLC$ circuit, when $X_C > X_L$, the inductive current will be greater than the capacitive current and the circuit is inductive.

✓ When $v$ and $i$ are both positive or both negative, *their product is positive and power is expended throughout the cycle.*

✓ If $v$ is negative while $i$ is positive during any part of the cycle, or if $i$ is negative while $v$ is positive, their product will be negative. *This "negative" power is not available for work and is returned to the line.*

✓ The power factor $PF$ determines what portion of the apparent power is real power and can vary from 1 when the phase angle is $0°$ to 0 when $\theta = 90°$.

# Solved Problems

**Solved Problem 7.1** Find the impedance and current of an *RLC* series circuit containing a number of series resistances and reactances (Figure 7-19).

**Figure 7-19** Series *RLC* circuit for ASP 7.1

**Solution:** Add the values of similar circuit elements.

Resistance: $\quad R_T = R_1 + R_2 = 10 + 15 = 25 \, \Omega$

Capacitance: $\quad X_{C,T} = X_{C1} + X_{C2} = 20 + 10 = 30 \, \Omega$

Inductance: $\quad X_{L,T} = X_{L1} + X_{L2} = 30 + 25 = 55 \, \Omega$

Net Reactance: $\quad X_T = X_{L,T} - X_{C,T} = 55 - 30 = 25 \, \Omega$

$$Z = \sqrt{R_T^2 + X_T^2} = \sqrt{25^2 + 25^2} = 35.4 \, \Omega$$

$$I = \frac{V_T}{Z} = \frac{100}{35.4} = 2.82 \text{ A}$$

**Solved Problem 7.2** A $30 - \Omega$ resistor, a $40 - \Omega$ inductive reactance and a $60 - \Omega$ capacitive reactance are connected in parallel across a

120-V 60-Hz ac line (Figure 7-20). Find $I_T, \theta, Z_T$, and $P$ . Is the circuit inductive or capacitive? Draw the current-phasor diagram.

**Figure 7-20** Parallel *RLC* circuit for Solved Problem 7.2

**Step 1:** Find $I_T$ and $\theta$.

$$I_R = \frac{V_T}{R} = \frac{120}{30} = 4 \text{ A} \qquad I_L = \frac{V_T}{X_L} = \frac{120}{40} = 3 \text{ A} \qquad I_C = \frac{V_T}{X_C} = \frac{120}{60} = 2 \text{ A}$$

Since $I_L > I_C$, the circuit is inductive.

$$I_T = \sqrt{I_R^2 + (I_L - I_C)^2} = \sqrt{4^2 + 1^2} = 4.12 \text{ A}$$

$$\theta = \arctan\left(-\frac{I_L - I_C}{I_R}\right) = \arctan\left(-\frac{1}{4}\right) = -14°$$

**Step 2:** Find $Z_T$.

$$Z_T = \frac{V_T}{I_T} = \frac{120}{4.12} = 29.1 \, \Omega$$

**Step 3:** Find $P$.

$$P = V_T I_T \cos\theta = 120(4.12)(\cos 14°) = 480 \text{ W}$$

or

$$P = I_R^2 R = 4^2(30) = 480 \text{ W}$$

**Step 4:** Draw the current-phasor diagram (Figure 7-21)

**Figure 7-21** Current-phasor diagram for Solved Problem 7.2

**Solved Problem 7.3** An ac motor operating at 75% *PF* draws 8 A from a 110-V ac line. Find the apparent and real power.

**Solution:**

Apparent power: $\qquad S = VI = 110(8) = 880$ VA

Real (true) power: $\qquad P = VI \cos\theta$

$$PF = \cos\theta = 0.75$$

$$P = 110(8)(.75) = 660 \text{ W}$$

**Solved Problem 7.4** A motor operating at 85% *PF* draws 300 W from a 120-V ac line. What is the current drawn?

**Solution:**

$$P = VI \cos\theta \quad \Rightarrow \quad I = \frac{P}{V \cos\theta} = \frac{300}{120(0.85)} = 2.94 \text{ A}$$

# Index